Economy, Society, and History

The Mises Institute dedicates this volume to all of its generous Supporters and wishes to thank these in particular:

Benefactors

Anonymous, in honor of Lew Rockwell, Steven R. Berger, Fernando Bernad
Colby Callahan, Remy Demarest, Thomas and Lisa Dierl
Jerry T. Dowell, in memory of Donald A. MacLennan
Joseph Edward Paul Melville, in memory of Harold Morris,
Clarice Melville Morris, and their son, Johnny Morris: The Gold Standard in this Life
Mr. and Mrs. Brian A. Miller
Akihiko Murai, in honor of all the people, known and unknown, who fight for Liberty
Mr. and Mrs. Gary J. Turpanjian
William P. Weidner, in honor of Hannah Gunderson

Patrons

Abdelhamid Abdou, Anonymous, John and Jan Brunner
Campbell Family Foundation, Mr. and Mrs. Raymond E. Cunningham
Dr. Ernest N. Curtis, in memory of Murray N. Rothbard, Jeffrey K. Czyz
Dr. David Dürr, Dr. Larry J. Eshelman, Matthew Gessner, T.J. and Ida Goss
Kevin R. Griffin, Wayne Harley, Juliana and Hunter Hastings
Hunter Lewis and Elizabeth Sidamon-Eristoff, Zoran Mitrovski, Patrick Moling
Gregory and Joy Morin, James Nardulli, Paul F. Peppard, top dog™
Chris and Melodie Rufer, Joseph Vierra, Mr. and Mrs. Fritz von Mering
Isaac James Waldron, Dr. J. Stanley Warford, Augustus Whitaker, Isaac Woerlen

Donors

Mr. and Mrs. David P. Abernathy, Lubor Adamek, Mr. and Mrs. J. Ryan Alford
Thomas Balmer, Dr. John Bartel, J. Duncan Berry PhD, Heinz Bitterli
Samuel Blackman, Herbert Borbe, Dr. Carlo Alberto Bosello, Matthew Bowler
Roman J. Bowser, James Bradley, Bryan Lee Briggs
John L. Buttolph, III, in memory of Murray N. Rothbard, Prof. Paul Cantor
David Capshaw, Dr. Andrew Carver, Christopher P. Casey, Jonathan Coe
Jean-Sylvain Cousin, Carl S. Creager, Helen B. Davis, Michael DeVinney, Paul J. Dietrich
J. Richard Duke, Dr. Dan Eisenberg, Trent Emberson, Eric Englund, Jason H. Fane
Ana Catarina Ferreira da Silva, Julian Fondren, David Franceschi
Mr. and Mrs. David Fusato, Randy Gann, Dietmar Georg, Christopher Georgacas
Dr. Dennis P. Gilman, in memory of Chesley and Lydia Gilman
Allen Gindler, in memory of my mother, Svetlana Glembocki, Dean Glover
Kevin P. Hamilton, in honor of those who still fight for Individual Liberty
Charles F. Hanes, Adam W. Hogan, Greg E. Hood, Terry Hulsey, Luis Felipe Karam Ludert
Dr. John A. Kasch, Franklin Keller, Dr. Matthias G. Kelm, Bernard and Joan Koether
Richard J. Kossmann, MD, Ganesh Kumar, Lemuel and Karul Lasher, Jeff Leskovar
Dr. Antonio A. Lloréns-Rivera, David L. March, Alexander Markesinis, Joseph H. Matarese
Herbert H. McAdams III, Paul McAvinney, Mark McGrath, Michael Merriman
Mark A. Monoscalco, Dr. Robert Montgomery, Martin Moško, Brandon Mueller
Allen Pegues, Jaan Pillesaar, Mr. and Mrs. Oscar Porcelli, Scott Richardson
Jorge F. Roca Arteta, Patrick Rosenwald, Thomas S. Ross, Dr. and Mrs. Murray Sabrin
Nicholas Sallnow-Smith, Dr. John H. Scacchia, Dr. William Seeger, Robert Seffrin
Brandon Shavers, Henri Etel Skinner, Petr Smidrkal, Keith and Darla Smith
Carlton M. Smith, Dr. James Speights, Mr. and Mrs. Michael Stack, Richard L. Stees
Dirck W. Storm, Zachary L. Tatum, Omar Torres, Thomas E. Verkuilen, Alexander Voss
Mr. and Mrs. James P. Walker, Mr. and Mrs. Donald F. Warmbier
Dr. Wayne Whitmore, Mr. and Mrs. Jerry Wynens

Economy, Society, and History

Hans-Hermann Hoppe

Published 2021 by the Mises Institute

Mises Institute
518 West Magnolia Avenue
Auburn, Ala. 36832
mises.org

ISBN: 978-1-61016-734-5

Contents

Foreword

One of the more depressing claims made by some libertarians during the past fifty years is that the battle for liberty is to be won or lost by arguing about economics. As with all but the grosser falsehoods, there is a degree of truth in the claim. Production and trade are important activities in any community. In those communities where debate over these things is possible and thought important, there tends to exist a power of coercion willing and able to act on the outcomes of such debate. For this reason, anyone worried about the establishment of state socialism and its great and terrible consequences needs a set of arguments that stand by themselves and that demonstrate both the evils of state control and the benefits of voluntary exchange.

But the claim that this is all we need remains depressing. Any movement that accepts it opens itself to entry and control by men of undoubtedly high intelligence, but whose preferred mode of reasoning is a wooden economism. Since most people cannot or do not choose to understand the less obvious truths of economics, this mode of reasoning will win no arguments outside those areas regarded as economic. Within those areas, it may become dominant. It may remain dominant there even after some variety of statism has become dominant in every other subject. But, as we have seen since the end of the Cold War, a grim and searching despotism is possible that has no interest in controlling the price of bread or in who owns the railways. A libertarian movement defined by the quality of its economic reasoning, and by nothing else, then becomes a waste of space.

This large and permanent truth—that libertarianism is more than an argument about economics—is what makes the work of Hans-Hermann Hoppe so important. If more than competent in economics, he is ultimately a philosopher with historical tastes. He stands in the same line as Adam Smith and Herbert Spencer. He is unusually qualified to appreciate and build on the work of his immediate masters, Murray Rothbard and Ludwig von Mises. We should particularly welcome this present book, which is a publication for the first time of lectures given almost a generation ago—lectures that were seen at the time as a profound contribution to the libertarian debate, lectures that the passage of time has shown to be not merely profound but also predictive. The approach taken by Hoppe is not that liberty is good because it lets us have cheaper electric toasters. His argument instead is that any defence of liberty is and must be identical to the defence of civilisation itself.

Though common till a few generations ago, talk nowadays of higher or lower states of development is out of fashion. Even so, human beings appear to be different from every other species on our planet because of our comparatively immense rational faculties and because of our physical mediocrity. No bodies as slow and weak and undefended as ours could have evolved without the compensations of intelligence—or, having evolved, could have survived. Equally important for our survival was the anatomy of our throats. Why this is as it is cannot be explained. But it allowed the development of language. This is what completed our separation from the other animals. Without language, we could have used our brains to keep ourselves and our children alive in small groups. With language, our physical need for cooperation set us on a path of capital accumulation that begins with teaching a child how to shape bones into fishhooks and may end with our self-transformation into what our ancestors would have regarded as demi-gods.

From language and cooperation, moreover, comes a stronger sense of property. This sense, as Hoppe shows (pp. 16–18), is not a consequence of our intelligence or any specific path of cultural development. It is natural to at least all the higher mammals. It is natural to very young children, even before they learn to speak or reason. The sense of property, though, is greatly enlarged and elaborated by the fact of our development. From this comes a tendency toward specialisation and a corresponding need to trade. Alongside this, the science of law has grown, as a means of ensuring property and enabling its peaceful transfer.

In any survey of our development, the obvious limitation is that we have no standard of comparison outside ourselves. Let us imagine that we are under observation by the sociologists and economists of some alien race. Is watching us a bored ticking of boxes? "Yes, they've finally discovered the plough. After a few millennia of wrong turns, they have alphabetic writing. They're making use of the electromagnetic spectrum, and have a crude nuclear technology. Next stop, either self-annihilation or meaningful life extension...." Is that us? Or should these hypothetical observers be sending frantic messages home, reporting some galactic miracle and asking for greater funding? It would be nice to know where we stand—assuming, that is, we are not alone and that talk of comparative development has any meaning. There is no doubt, however, that we existed in something like our present shape as a race of illiterate hunter-gatherers for several hundred thousand years until the end of the last ice age, just ten thousand years ago. Since then, we have grown from a few million to seven billion, and the majority of this growth has happened since the birth of many people who are still alive. Since it could not have happened by itself, we can take this expansion of numbers as a measurement of our overall progress.

Yet, though impressive—whether we imagine some group of excited alien observers, or just look how we did until the end of the last ice age—there is a worm in the bud of our progress. The generality of our achievement in the past ten thousand years has come about from private interest and free exchange. This is not to say that force has been absent or even unnecessary. All civilisation needs defensive force. Individuals need to defend themselves and their dependants from thieves and other low parasites. Communities need to defend themselves from organised bands of those who get their living from consuming what they have not produced. Between these two extremes, there is a need for courts to rule on the nature and fulfilment of contracts, and for their decisions to be enforced against non-consenting losers in the judicial game. In short, every community must have a place for defensive force, and much of this defensive force will be collective. But if force has not been, and could not be, absent from our progress, how much of this force needed to be coercive?

The answer for Hoppe, and for every other principled libertarian, is none. Private interest and free exchange are all that is needed to take us from the mud to the stars. So far as it is needed, defensive force can be as easily provided from within a voluntary system, as good bread and clean water can be provided. There is no utility in allowing the emergence of "one agency, and only one agency, the state … [having] the right to tax and to ultimate decision-making (p. 179). Our greatest error as a species has been, time after time, to allow the emergence of these agencies of armed coercion. Until the twentieth century, states were limited in the harm they might do by the poverty of their host communities. They might rob and murder on a scale that still appals. At the same time, the number of direct parasites was hardly ever out of four figures, and the number of their exclusive clients always hard to keep near the top of five figures. Also, if they could rob and murder, their powers of more detailed inspection and control were limited in ways we often no longer understand.

Our misfortune in the past hundred years is that greater wealth has meant greater taxable capacity, and therefore an almost unlimited growth in the size of states and in the numbers of the parasites they support. There is probably no point in describing the malicious freakishness of the modern state in America or Britain. On the one hand, I live in England and earn some of my bread from an institution funded by the British state. It would be unwise to say all that I think. On the other hand, this is not only a malicious but a metastatic freakishness. Whatever sounds bizarre today will border on normality compared with whatever is in fashion a year from today.

Hoppe has no easy comfort to dispense here. Indeed, part of his analysis is as bleak as that of any English Tory after 1945. If an individual makes a mistake, he will tend eventually to be aware that he has made a mistake and either to correct it or to wish he had corrected it in time. At the worst, his example will stand as a warning to others. In the natural sciences, mistakes tend to be self-limiting—they will lead to falsified predictions, and these will be followed by a re-examination of the alleged facts. But, when the wrong turn is made into statism,

> not everyone holding this error must pay for it equally. Rather, some people will have to pay for the error, while others, maybe the agents of the state, actually benefit from the same error. Because of this, in this case, it would be mistaken to assume that there exists a universal desire to learn and to correct one's error. Quite to the contrary, in this case, it will have to be assumed

> that some people instead of learning and promoting the truth, actually have a constant motive to lie, that is, to maintain and promote falsehoods, even if they themselves recognize them as such. (p. 180)

Of course, the politicians themselves are among the main villains here. Perhaps more to blame, though, are the intellectuals. These have a compelling and permanent interest in spreading the falsehood of state necessity.

> The market demand for intellectual services, in particular in the area of the humanities and the social sciences, is not exactly high and also not exactly stable and secure. Intellectuals would be at the mercy of the values and choices of the masses and the masses are generally uninterested in intellectual and philosophical concerns. The state, on the other hand, as Rothbard has noted, accommodates their typically overinflated egos and is willing to offer the intellectuals a warm, secure, and permanent berth in its apparatus, a secure income and the panoply of prestige. And indeed, the modern democratic state in particular has created a massive oversupply of intellectuals. (pp. 182–83)

On the other hand, there is hope. What this is I leave you to find out for yourself by reading Hoppe's lectures. They say more than I can in this foreword. If I must give a teaser, though, all statism is malevolence and rests ultimately on the consent of the oppressed. Let the eyes of the oppressed be opened, and there will be no more statism. Eyes will not be opened by the wooden economising of my second paragraph. They will be opened by a study of history and anthropology to which these essays can be taken as an introduction.

Sean Gabb
Deal, England
June 2021

Preface

In June 2004, at the invitation of Lew Rockwell, I spent one week at the Mises Institute in Auburn, Alabama, to present a series of lectures: one in the morning and one in the afternoon, for five days, in an intimate setting, before a live audience of some fifty plus students and professionals.

The goal, as set by Lew Rockwell, was an ambitious one: to present my view of the world and its inner workings. Accordingly, the lectures were to be a wide-ranging, interdisciplinary intellectual endeavor, touching upon questions of philosophy, economics, anthropology, sociology, and history.

My lectures were not based on a written text, but on notes, supplemented by only a few handouts. Hence, the somewhat informal tone of the following text and its occasional personal and conversational asides. Based on personal experience I do not expect this fact to diminish but rather to actually enhance the appeal and accessibility of the present work, however, and thus felt no need now for any stylistic changes.

As well, I came to the same conclusion not just regarding style but substance as well. It is nearly twenty years ago now that I presented the following lectures. They were audio taped at the time and a CD was produced. But I never looked back nor listened to these recordings. Indeed, I hardly ever listen to recordings of my own speeches, and in general, insofar as intellectual rather than theatrical or artistic matters are concerned, I much prefer the written over the spoken word. Revisiting now, for the first time, in its written form what I had orally presented in 2004, then, I was quite pleasantly surprised and reached the conclusion that I should not fiddle around with anything but let everything stand as is. This is not to say, of course, that there is nothing more to say about the wide-ranging subject matters of the following work, but rather, if I may be so immodest to say so, that it is a remarkably solid stepping-stone for more and better things still hopefully to come.

As a matter of fact, I have not stopped reading, writing, and lecturing myself since 2004, and the curious reader may already find quite a few additional observations, considerations, and deliberations in my own subsequent works, replete with further references. Among others, there is the second, expanded edition of *The Economics and Ethics of Private Property* (2006), *A Short History of Man* (2015), *Getting Libertarianism Right* (2018) and, most recently, the second, greatly expanded edition of *The Great Fiction* (2021). As well, those preferring things live and in color may want to take a look at some of the many video recordings made of my speeches in recent years, most notably my regular presentations at the annual Property and Freedom Society (PFS) meetings, all of which are electronically available on my personal home page, www.HansHoppe.com.

Finally, the reader may find it of interest to learn a bit about the personal circumstances and the temporal-historical context, in which the present work should be placed. As briefly mentioned in lecture four, when I presented my lectures, in June of 2004, I was in the middle of some major trouble with UNLV, my university. A student had accused me of having violated some standard of "political correctness" and thus creating a "hostile learning environment" for him, and the university had thereupon initiated an official investigation into the matter that would drag on for almost another year. Afterward, in 2005, I told the whole sordid story in an article titled "My Battle with the Thought Police."[1] Yet while I ultimately emerged triumphant

---

[1] Hans-Hermann Hoppe, "My Battle with the Thought Police," *Mises Daily*, April 12, 2005, https://mises.org/library/my-battle-thought-police.

from the scandalous affair, it had some lasting impact on my life. Not only had one year of my life been stolen from me as a result, but I had lost much of my former enthusiasm as a teacher and my appreciation of academic life. I had seen ominous signs of the increasing spread of "political correctness" all throughout society before, of course, but I felt myself immune from this, in my eyes, mental disease. In my teaching, I had recognized and accepted no intellectual taboo whatsoever, and, whether because or despite of this, I had enjoyed great popularity among my students. All the while, in my position as a tenured, full professor, I had considered myself well protected by my university from any and all interference with academic freedom. This belief had been severely shattered, and in light of an increasing number of similar events at other universities around the country at the same time, I came to the realization that for me, with my wide-ranging, interdisciplinary intellectual interests, university teaching henceforth would always mean having to choose between self-censorship, on the one hand, or harassment on the other.

Luckily, I was to be quickly rescued from this dilemma by some fortunate turn in my personal life, however, that allowed me to resign from my university position and continue my scholarly work outside of official academia. Looking back now, I would say "just in time," because matters only got worse, and rapidly so. During my student days, in Germany, universities constituted to a large extent still anarchic orders made up of dozens of little autonomous intellectual kingdoms and fiefdoms, freely competing or cooperating with each other, and university students made up no more than 7 or 8 percent of an age group. Since then, universities have been increasingly transformed into huge, highly centralized organizations, ruled by a central committee of bureaucrats and a steadily growing mass of administrative assistants, while students now, in the US, make up more than 50 percent of an age group. Under these circumstances, with a bureaucratic central committee in charge, and whether by commission or omission, universities, then, pressured by so-called anti-fascist student mobs and Black Lives Matter hoodlums and egged on therein by some professorial frauds, fakes and fools thus catapulted to public prominence, have been increasingly turned into indoctrination camps of "political correctness," or "wokeness," as defined by a few theoreticians of "cultural

Marxism." And not quite unlike Mao's erstwhile cultural revolution with its Red Guards, then, this wokeness movement has made great strides toward its goal of subverting and ultimately destroying all traditional Western standards of human excellence, merit, achievement and, indeed, normality and all things normal, and silencing, ousting or beating into submission anyone daring to dissent from the one and only correct, woke political party line.

Today, in contemporary university, in the US, the UK, Germany, and many other Western countries, then, many things said or noted in the following can no longer be said or noted without fear of serious repercussions: without open calls for cancellation, censorship, apology, confession of guilt or even harassment, threat and loss of job and livelihood. The more reason, then, to thank Lew Rockwell, the Mises Institute, and in particular the many generous donors, who have made the present publication possible.

Hans-Hermann Hoppe
May 2021

LECTURE 1

The Nature of Man and the Human Condition: Language, Property, and Production

---

What I want to do in this seminar is to reconstruct world history from the bottom up, from the beginning of mankind to the present, and gradually enlarge and expand the picture. I will give you a brief overview of what I have planned, but let me say from the outset that I have never given these lectures in this form before. I have presented some of these topics in various lectures, and in my class on comparative systems I talk about subjects similar to the subjects that I will deal with in this seminar. But never before have I presented lectures structured in this way.

To give you some basic idea as to how this whole thing is structured, in the first lecture I want to talk about the nature of man, comparing men with animals and illuminating the major differences, and characterizing what one can call the human condition, the condition that mankind finds itself confronted with. In the second lecture, I will talk about the spread of humans across the globe and the development, i.e., the *extensification* and the *intensification*, of the division of labor. And the third lecture deals with the next element in human and economic development, that is, the development of money and the expansion of the use of money and the consequences that money has for the development of the division of labor. The next fundamental element, lecture four, will be the theory of time preference, and of capital and technology, and of economic growth.

All of the lectures, by the way, will contain theoretical elements as well as historical elements. I am not a historian by profession. My advantage is that I know more theory than most historians, and because of that I reconstruct history in a slightly different way than a historian might do it.

The fifth lecture will deal with ideological factors that have an influence on social and economic development, that is, in particular, religion; this will be a lecture on comparative religions and comparative ideologies. Lecture six will be dealing with details of the theory of private property and the issue of how societies would defend property, i.e., property rights, with special reference to feudal societies and what defense mechanisms would be used in modern societies where we can take some ideas from the feudal age. In lecture seven we will deal with parasitic behavior, that is, exploitative behavior and the origin of the state. And lecture eight will be based on something that I have done in my book *Democracy: The God That Failed*, discussing the transition from monarchical states or monarchical governments to democratic governments. Lecture nine will deal with states and imperialism and war. And the final lecture will address some strategic issues; that is, how do we go from here to a society that is free, or at least more free than the current one.

So, with this, let me begin to talk about the nature of man and the human condition and speak in particular about three elements that are unique to mankind. First is language, the second is property, and the third is production or technology. Now, you realize that when we begin all of this here, we are already talking. We are already using some of our capabilities, some of our skills and achievements that are the result of human evolution; that is, the reconstruction that I will offer of human history already makes use of some of the tools that have only gradually evolved in the course of time. Actually, the origin of language is dated back roughly to somewhere between 150,000 and 50,000 years ago. All of these estimates are, of course, as you can imagine, rather vague;

nobody was around at that time to record exactly when they started talking. But these are the numbers that some geneticists and biologists and anthropologists give us for the beginning. And you will notice something else, from the fact that we begin all of this enterprise by talking to each other, that humans are social animals.

You are aware of the fact that there are people who are interested in game theory, for instance, who seem to have trouble sometimes explaining why people cooperate at all and do not fight each other all the time. But the funny thing is that this debate already takes place using language, which, in a way, from the outset, explains that there must be something wrong with this idea that mankind at some point was, so to speak, deciding whether they should fight each other or whether they should not fight each other. Obviously, as soon as mankind began to talk with each other, they must have already recognized that there are certain advantages to doing this and to being social in one's endeavors. And it's perfectly clear from the outset what the great advantage is of having a language available and communicating with other people, since we can convey knowledge to other people in a much faster way than would be possible if we simply had to look at what other people are doing and then try to reconstruct the ideas that are behind what they are doing. Through the use of language we have the possibility of communicating directly what it was that led us to do this or led us to do something else.

Now, with language, two ideas emerged and I use here the ideas that were developed first by an Austrian psychologist, Karl Bühler, who also had some influence on Karl Popper, who uses his ideas. Karl Bühler makes the point that when we look at language, we can distinguish between four different functions, two of which we find already on the animal level and two of which are unique to humans. On the animal level, we find the use of symbols or sounds that express something like pain, for instance. That is an *expressive function* of language, which we can ascribe easily also to animals and say, in this sense, that they can express some internal feelings. On the other hand, language has sometimes a *signal function*; that is, we can produce sounds that indicate there is some danger coming, warn other animals to run away, or something like this. And this, of course, is also possible for humans to do. Language has an expressive function for us and also has this signal function, to make other people aware of things.

What is not found in the animal kingdom is language that has a *descriptive* function; that is, language that describes, "this is such and such" and with the descriptive function of language, for the first time, the idea of truth emerges. That is, for expressions and signals, whether that is true or not is not really an issue, but when we say, "this is such and such," then it becomes possible to ask, "Is that really the case?," and we can try to find out whether this is the case or not. So, the idea of tools comes into being, because language has a descriptive function and the most primitive descriptive propositions would be of the type "this is such and such"; that is, having a proper name or an identifying expression, and then a general term characterizing a particular object as having some general characteristics.

The second unique human function of language is the *argumentative* function, that we have complex statements connected by "and" and "or," several statements combined with each other, and that we investigate whether certain arguments are valid or not and investigate whether we draw inferences in the correct way or incorrect way and so forth. And you realize that it is precisely this last function, this argumentative function, that we must also use as a tool, if we now want to make a more precise distinction between the abilities of man on the one hand and the different abilities of animals on the other.

And I want to follow here with philosopher Brand Blanshard, who has pointed out some important differences between animals and humans. I want to begin with a short quote from Blanshard in a book, *Reason and Analysis*, where he says this about animals and then draws a conclusion that this is somehow still very different from what mankind can do. He asks, "What does it mean to have human reason or human rationality?" And he answers, "It cannot be consciousness, of course, because no one can sensibly doubt that animals feel fear and hunger and pleasure and pain." Animals can also make mistakes, which we recognize, as when, for instance, a dog drops a bone for a more inviting bone that he sees in the water. And since only judgments can be mistaken, animals must also in some way be able to make judgments to come to the conclusion that "I made a wrong judgment." And since judgment is thought, we can also say that animals think, but they do, obviously, not think in the same way as humans do.

Now, what is the difference between our way of thinking and their way of thinking? Let me emphasize four points in this connection which partly overlap. The first thing to be noted is that animal thought is always tied to perception, whereas human thought can wander around, go back to the past, wander to the future, can think about objects that are far away, can even think about objects that have never existed. Animals cannot think in this way. Whatever they're thinking, it requires some present cue, some observation from which their thinking arises. We can imagine, for instance, that animals can also think, to a certain extent, about things that are absent, as if a dog sits in front of a house because the dog knows that his master has gone into the house and waits there patiently until the master comes back out. But even there you can still see that it is tied to perception. If he had not seen the master go into the house, he would not do what he does, sitting there waiting. And in any case, he cannot think about things that are far away, or impossible, or things in the far distant future. So, that's the first thing: animal thought is tied to perception and human thought is, in this way, freed up from perception.

That brings me to the second point. There is one other phenomenon, the difference between humans and animals, that shows they cannot do this. Even if you think they might think about this sort of stuff, they have no way of conveying this type of information to us. Or you can say, animals can't abstract in the way that humans can abstract. Certainly, animals can see shapes and colors and they can perceive smells and things like this, but it doesn't seem to be the case that they have a concept of shapes, of triangles, or a concept of green or blue or yellow, or a concept of different types of smells. Again, this is an aspect of what I just mentioned; it is tied to specific events, but they cannot abstract from the specific event and build a general concept. If they could, then we would expect them to form a word for these things, and it is not that animals are not capable of producing sounds. Many animals do have the equipment to produce sounds. So, this does not explain why they don't have words. Obviously, despite the fact that they can form sounds, they cannot form what we refer to as words, sounds to which we attach a certain abstract idea of which we find various instances in the real world.

The third thing that distinguishes mankind from animals is that animals cannot make explicit inferences. Again, this has something intimately to do with the two points that I already made. Animals can, of course, make inferences, but these inferences are implicit. That is to say, if you have a chicken and you give a piece of food to the chicken that is too big, doesn't fit into its mouth, and it is desperate that it can't eat it. Then, if you throw another piece of roughly the same size in front of it, the chicken might refuse to even try to do the same with the second piece of material because it recognizes that it didn't work with the first, it's not likely to work with the second. But again, due to the lack of concepts, they cannot make explicit inferences; that is, infer from one concept to another and thereby be able to say why such-and-such caused such-and-such a problem and why it would be in vain to try the same thing twice that already didn't work in the first case.

The most important difference between animals and humans is the fact that animals do not have what we call self-consciousness. They do have consciousness, but not self-consciousness, and what I mean by self-consciousness is that they cannot mentally stand back and reflect on their own behavior. They cannot pause and criticize their own behavior, think about why their behavior was successful or unsuccessful. They do not have anything like norms or principles against which they can judge their own behavior and criticize their own behavior. Let me on this point again quote Blanshard on this most important of differences, that is, the human capacity for self-conscious reflection. There he says,

> Finally, human reason has added an extra dimension to the animal consciousness in the form of self-consciousness. An animal lacks the power, which is the source in ourselves, of so much achievement and so much woe, of standing off from itself and contemplating what it is doing. It eats, sleeps and cavorts, but never pauses in the midst of a meal, to take note that it's eating greedily, never asks, was it not unseemly to sleep the hours away…[1]

[1]Brand Blanshard, *Reason and Analysis* (1962; Abingdon, UK: Routledge, 2013), chap. 2, p. 51.

You see, in some respects, of course, humans have not developed that far beyond.

> ...apparently, never reflects, as it leaps and runs, that it is a little off-form today. It makes mistakes, but having made one, it cannot sit down and consider what principle of right thinking is violated. Because it cannot contemplate its own behavior it cannot criticize itself; being below the level of self-criticism, it has no norms; and having no norms, it lacks one great obvious essential to the life of reason, namely, the power to be guided by principle.[2]

And Blanshard then summarizes all of what I tried to convey up to this point, by saying the following:

> When we say that man is a rational animal, then, we seem to imply that he can command ideas independently of sense, independently of perception, that he can abstract; that he can infer explicitly and that he can sit in judgment on himself. The highest of animals can do none of these things. The stupidest of man, if not a pathological case, can in some measure do them all.[3]

So much about the human ability, the human language ability, is characterized in particular by our abilities of self-reflection, self-criticism, self-control, and so forth.

These capabilities we can now use in order to describe the human condition, which will be my next step. And this human condition can be characterized in the following way: mankind finds itself equipped with consciousness, and discovers that we have a physical body, and discovers that there is something outside of the physical body, what economists call "land," that is, nature-given resources, things outside, independent of our bodies. And what we learn immediately is that our bodies are constantly and permanently pressed by various needs, and

---

[2]Ibid.

[3]Ibid.

that we have to act in order to satisfy these needs. What man immediately discovers is that certain things he can control directly; that is, we can all discover that we can directly control our own bodies. I can just say "I lift my arm" and my arm is lifted, or "I lift my leg" and my leg will go up. And we realize that nobody else can control my body this way.

Everybody can do that with his own body, of course, but we have this ability of directly controlling something only with very limited things. I cannot control you directly; I can only control you by being in direct control of my own physical body first; then I can, of course, make an indirect attempt to also control you. This explains why we have the concept of *I*, of *me*, because certain things only I can do, and that distinguishes me from the outset from everybody else. This is what I can do and nobody can do this to my arm in the way I can do it. We can also say that we discover then, immediately, what we mean by having a *free will*. I can just want this; I just pick this up and that's it. There's nothing that forces me; it's just my own wanting it, so that makes it so. And we also develop, immediately, some sort of idea of what it means to cause something. I am the cause of this bottle of water being in my hand and I am the cause of now drinking out of it. We recognize our unique relationship that we have to our own physical body and that other people have to their own physical bodies. We know that because of this, *I am not you, and you are not me*. We understand the concept of cause and we understand the concept of free will. Then we recognize, second, that there are other things out there that we can only control indirectly, with the help of those things that we can control directly. With the help of our body, we can attempt to control things that exist external to our own physical body. We refer to those things as *means*.

And we realize also that there exist things that we cannot control at all. We cannot control sunshine or rain; we cannot control the movement of the moon or the stars. Those things we refer to as the *environment*, which we have to take as a given, as something that is beyond our control. The borderline between those things that we can control and those things that we cannot control, the borderline, so to speak, between those that are means and what is the environment in which we act, is moveable; that is, certain things might come within our reach and can become controllable that were initially not controllable.

Just think of something simple like building a tool, for instance, that makes it possible for you to reach something up high that you initially couldn't, or reach heights that you could initially not reach, or down to depths that you initially could not reach. The borderline between the range of objects that become means and the range of objects that remain environment, this boundary is movable or flexible. It might well be the case that one day, we will be able to just move the moon around by waving certain types of tools or instruments, but currently we are not able to do so.

Then, man learns that some of the means, some of the things that he can control, that he can move, that he can manipulate, can be referred to as "goods" and others can be referred to as "bads." *Goods* would obviously be those means that are suitable in order to satisfy some needs that we have, and *bads* would be objects that we can control, but that would have negative repercussions on us, that would not satisfy any needs but, to the contrary, may harm us or even kill us.

At this point, let me read you the definition of goods. "Goods" are means that can be controlled and which are suitable for the satisfaction of human needs or ends. I will give you the definition that Carl Menger provided us with. Menger pointed out that there are four requirements for objects to become goods for us. The first is the existence of a human need. The second requirement is such properties as render the thing capable of being brought into a causal connection with a satisfaction of this need. That is, this object must be capable, through our performing certain manipulations with it, to cause certain needs to be satisfied or at least relieved. The third condition is that there must be human knowledge about this connection, which explains, of course, why it is important for people to learn to distinguish between *goods* and *bads*. Thus, we have human knowledge about the object, our ability to control it, and the causal power of this object to lead to certain types of satisfactory results. And the fourth factor is, as I already indicated, that we must have command of the thing sufficient to direct it to the satisfaction of the need. In this sense, for instance, even though we might consider sunshine to be a good or rain to be a good, neither would be an economic good, because we have no control over the objects that are capable of producing sunlight or rain. Only objects that we can bring under our control, and then lead to certain results, would be referred to as economic goods. Man then learns that some goods are immediately useful. We refer to those goods as *consumer goods*. They can be appropriated and almost instantly turned into some form of satisfaction. And we also learn that most things, however, are only indirectly useful. They require that we must transform them in some way, that we reshape them in some way, that we move or relocate them in some way, using our intelligence in order to lead to satisfaction. And those objects that we have to do something intelligent to, before they lead to satisfaction, we would call *producer goods*.

And man also recognizes—and this brings me to my second main point—besides language, the concept of *property*. I already made the point with respect to our physical bodies, where it is intuitively clear that people recognize that "this is my body, because I am the only one who can do this with it and nobody else can." I have a unique relationship to my body, a relationship unlike what anybody else has. When it comes now to economic means, a similar idea arises. Those people who appropriate certain objects, and bring them under their control in order to satisfy certain desires, have thereby also, of course, established a unique relationship to those things that they have appropriated for the first time, and they consider those things also theirs. Maybe not in the same direct way as with my body, but as an extension of my body. I used, after all, my body in order to appropriate these things and in this sense I have a unique relationship with these objects as well. Let me read to you, in this connection, a quote from Herbert Spencer, who also explains the naturalness of the idea of property. He says

> that even intelligent animals display a sense of proprietorship, negating the belief propounded by some that individual property was not recognized by primitive man. When we see the claim to exclusive possession understood by a dog, so that he fights in defense of his master's clothes, if left in charge of them, it becomes impossible to suppose that even in their lowest state, men were devoid of those ideas and emotions, which initiate private ownership. All that may be fairly

> assumed is, that these ideas and sentiments were first less developed than they have since become.[4]

While in the early stages, it is difficult, not to say impossible, to establish a mark of individual claims to part of the area wandered over in search of food—and I'll come to that subject later on in a future lecture—it is not difficult to mark off the claims to moveable things and to habitations, and these claims we find habitually recognized.

It is perfectly clear that moveable objects, tools, and so forth that people have were at all times recognized as their private property in those objects. In the most primitive of men, the concept of private property exists, not only with respect to his physical body, but also with respect to those appropriated means of production that indirectly satisfied his various desires.

Now let me elaborate a little bit on this concept of property by introducing a second person, call him Friday, and then, you recall, we are already talking with each other, so we have to assume that these types of Fridays existed from the very outset of mankind. With a second person present, it becomes possible that conflicts over scarce goods can arise. It is not possible that conflicts arise over things that are in superabundance, or that conflicts arise with regard to events caused by the environment. We cannot influence the environment, and if there exists a superabundance of goods, then it is possible that people may have different ideas of what should be done or should not be done with a good, because whatever I do, it doesn't affect what other people can do with the same type of good, because it simply exists in superabundance.

From the most primitive stages of mankind on, what people recognize is how to solve these possible conflicts with regard to scarce resources. They will point out that, "Look, I have an objective, perceivable, noticeable connection to such and such a thing, because I have appropriated it, I have control over it, I have used it for this type of purpose, and I have all of this done before you ever came along and wanted to do something with the same object. So, my claim is better justified than yours. As a matter of fact, your claim is not justified at

[4]Herbert Spencer, *Principles of Sociology*, 2d ed. (New York: D. Appleton Co., 1916), vol. 2, p. 538.

all, because you cannot point to any objective link established between your body and a particular object, whereas I can point to a particular visible, noticeable, intersubjectively ascertainable link between me and a particular object."

We can recognize this by the fact that people are, again, from the most primitive stages on, willing to defend these objects from invasions by other people. If I were not willing to defend something, if I do not put up the slightest resistance against somebody taking my axe or my arrow, then I indicate, in a way, that I do not consider it to be my property. If I show the slightest resistance, saying no or pushing my hands in the direction of the person trying to take it away from me, this indicates clearly that I regard myself as being the owner and having a special control over these things. Again, we can see this if we look at small children. If they have disputes over whose toy this is, the typical response of children is to say, "Look, I'm already playing with the car and you are not." And if they put absolutely no resistance up, then they indicate that, for the time being, they have abandoned it and made it available to others. So again, very primitive sentiments. In this sense, we can probably assume that the development of children, in a way, repeats, to a certain extent, the development of mankind as a whole. What we find in children, we also find already in primitive man.

Now, let me come to the third unique capability of mankind, besides language and the recognition of property. That is that man can produce things, that man is a producer, that he's capable of developing technology. You realize that animals live, so to speak, a parasitic life, in the sense that they never enhance the endowment of the world. They eat something, and in a way, diminish the amount of things that are available on Earth, but they never add anything to it.

Mankind is unique in the sense that they have, as compared with most animals, a distinctive lack of specialized organs and of instincts, which makes them basically incapable of survival unless they develop substitutes for this lack of natural equipment that they have. Men have no natural weapons with which to defend themselves, or nothing to speak of. We have practically no instincts that guide us automatically to do this and that and avoid this and recognize dangers without having to know about it. What we can say is that man needs culture in order to survive in nature.

And the tools, the most important tools that man has, are, on the one hand, his hands and, on the other hand, of course, his brain. But, neither one of these tools can be described as a highly specialized tool. They are useful for a wide variety of purposes, which is an advantage, but it is also obviously a disadvantage to begin with. We just have to learn what we can do with our hands and don't automatically know what our hands can possibly do and we have to learn what our brain is capable of doing and do not automatically, like most animals, know to what uses to put our brainpower. Men must then intelligently transform nature, by using brains and hands in particular. There are certain patterns in the development of technology that we can perceive if we look at the development of mankind as a whole.

Here I follow a German sociologist and anthropologist, Arnold Gehlen, whom I recommend quite highly. I think one of his books has also been translated into English. It's called, simply, *Man*, I believe. Gehlen does not have a very good reputation, because he had some sort of connection with the Nazis. But that does not make his observations any less important. So, he points out that there are attempts during our technological development to substitute for the lack of organs that we have. Then, technology serves a purpose of relieving us of insufficient capabilities, and then it has the tendency of strengthening our nature-given capabilities. Let me read you a quote from him (the quote is in German, so I have to ad lib here a little bit, in translating):

> Man is, in every natural environment, incapable of survival and because of this needs culture due to a lack of specialized organs and instincts. Without an environment that is specific to his species, in which he would fit in, without inborn purposeful behavior and behavioral patterns due to a lack of specific organs and instincts, with less than perfectly formed senses, without any weapons, naked in his *habitus embryonic*, insecure in his instincts, he must rely on action and on intelligent transformation of those circumstances that he happens to find.
>
> Hands and brains might be considered to be specialized organs of man, but they are specialized in a

> different sense than animal organs are. They can be used for many purposes. They are specialized for unspecialized purposes and achievements and they are, because of that, suitable for unpredictable circumstances arising in the world. The culture of primitive people, thus, consists first of its weapons in their tools, in their huts, in their animals and gardens, all of which is changed, transformed, cultivated, that is, by newly formed nature, by intelligent action.[5]

The first achievements of men are substitutes for lacking organs, weapons, for instance. Also, fire, as some form of natural protection and shelter.

The second type of tools that are developed are developed in order to strengthen naturally given abilities, like using stones in order to strengthen the power that a fist has, for instance, or hammers as tools that strengthen natural given powers, or microscopes, as instruments that are more developed than the natural human organs, eyes, or telephones as instruments that strengthen and surpass the natural given abilities that we have through our ears. And then he points out that there exist techniques that relieve humans by saving them labor. For instance, a wheeled wagon, which allows us to carry weights that we could not carry naturally, and instruments that even combine all of these things, that is, they are in some sense, substitutes for lacking things, in some respects surpassing natural abilities and in some sense relieving us, saving us labor that otherwise would be necessary, for instance, an airplane. An airplane allows us to fly, which unaided we cannot do at all. It surpasses all natural abilities that exist in this regard, and it takes work away completely insofar as it transports us, without any effort on our own part, from one place to another.

And Gehlen also points out that there exists in the history of technological development another tendency that we can recognize, and that is a gradual substitution of inorganic materials and forces for organic materials and forces. Initially, we used stone and wood and bone. The

---

[5]Quoted from Arnold Gehlen, *Anthropologische Forschung* (Hamburg: Rowohlt, 1965), pp. 94–95.

Stone Age ends roughly 8,000 years ago and then in the next stage, we already create some sort of artificial materials, bronze out of copper and tin, that begins roughly at 4,000 BC, or on the North American continent, only about 1,000 years ago. And then the next material, again, already further removed from the nature-given materials, would be iron, which comes into use around 1,200 BC, roughly, and then of course, finally, steel, which is a development of our relatively recent past. Instead of organic materials, we increasingly use cement and metals and coal. All of these things replace wood as burning material. We use steel ropes in order to replace leather and hemp ropes. We use synthetic colors instead of natural coloring materials. We increasingly use synthetic medicines instead of natural herbs, and so forth, and we make ourselves successively independent of natural energy sources.

For a long time, mankind was dependent on his naturally available energy sources, on forests growing up again. And the natural speed of trees growing up put a limitation on the speed of development that mankind could take. They were also dependent on natural, physical forces, such as the power of horses and oxen and things like this, which also could not be deliberately enlarged or empowered. And in the development of technology, gradually, we strip ourselves of these limitations by using first, coal and oil and then also water power and then of course, finally, atomic forces, which make us essentially independent of the growth of natural materials.

To conclude, let me quote again from Gehlen, who sees a logic in the development of human technology, a logic that we can see only if we look back from the present. In the past, we would not have been able, probably at the beginning of mankind, to predict that these would be the stages that technological development would go through, but looking backward, we can somehow understand that there was a certain inherent logic at work. He says,

> This process of technological development has three stages. On the first stage, that of the tool, the force necessary for work and the necessary mental effort, still have to be done by the human subject itself. The tools somehow make it easier for us, the strengthen our forces, give us more force than we normally have, and

reduce somehow the mental effort that is necessary, that we have to perform in conducting certain tasks. And in the second stage of the machine, steam engine and cars and so forth, the physical force is already technically *objectivated*; that means we don't need any force anymore on our own part; all the force is generated by the machines. And finally, on the third stage of technological development, which is that of the *automaton*, even the mental effort that the subject had to show in the previous stages becomes unnecessary or of very minor importance. And with each of these three stages, the instrument, the tool, the machine, and then finally, the automaton, the objectivation of the fulfillment of the purposes of technology comes closer to its ultimate purpose, and in the automaton, it is finally reached because we can do things without our physical or mental contribution.[6]

[6]Ibid.

LECTURE 2

The Spread of Humans around the World: The Extension and Intensification of the Division of Labor

IN THIS LECTURE,[1] I WANT to talk about the spread of humans around the world and the *extension* and the *intensification* of the division of labor. The subject will be continued to a certain extent into the next

[1] [This lecture began with two personal notes from Hoppe. While not directly related to the lecture, they are of historical value and interest. —Ed.]

First, let me make a few personal remarks. One is, since some of you have seen the videotape with Murray Rothbard, I should mention that for the last ten years of his life, I was his closest colleague. In a way, I was his intellectual bodyguard. I came to the United States in 1985 and worked with Murray for a year in New York City, and when he was out of town I taught his classes. And then in 1986, he received an offer for an endowed chair at the University of Nevada, Las Vegas, which was the first big position that he ever held. At that time, there was another opening as well, and he asked me to come with him. And by accident, I got that job too. It was, I think, the only year at that university where it was possible for both of us to be hired. From that

lecture. *Homo sapiens*, mankind as we know it, with about the cranial volume that we have now, is estimated to be about 500,000 years old, and takes on the current appearance roughly about 100,000 years ago. And as I mentioned in the previous lecture, the point when the language capability developed, is dated somehow from between 150,000 to 50,000 years ago. There is general agreement, not complete agreement, but pretty much unanimous agreement, that mankind spread out from Africa, and if you take a look at Figure 1, which is taken from the Cavalli-Sforza book, he gives you some rough dates about this process. So, his estimation is that people began to leave Africa 60,000–70,000 years ago, maybe up to 100,000 years ago, and that the first spreading was to Asia. We have the oldest findings of human skeletons, in China, dated at 67,000 years old.

And then, from China, they traveled to Australia, which he dates roughly at 55,000 years ago. And this travel time—I will have more to say about that—took about 10,000 years from Africa to Australia. One will have to say here something about the possibilities of this traveling. You have to keep in mind a few glacial periods, actually four glacial periods in the last 900,000 years and each of those lasted about 75,000 years. The last one of these glacial periods lasted from 25,000 years to about 13,000 years ago. During these glacial periods the level of the oceans dropped considerably because snow accumulated on the mountains and less water melted, so that the gaps between Southeast Asia and what is now Indonesia and Borneo and Australia became rather small. They did not disappear completely, but they were small enough that they could be traversed by very small boats. The Sahara Desert, for instance, is only 3,000 years old. Before that, it was not exactly the

moment on, the composition of the department changed in such a way that we never again would have received the jobs. Then I stayed there until he died in 1995, and now I'm the only lonely holdout there, one they can no longer get rid of.

The other remark concerns the lectures. The structure of the lectures is supposed to be the structure of my next book project. Because of that, in a way, I put more work into it than you normally tend to do. And on top of that, it is Lew Rockwell who, by inviting me, always forces me to overcome my natural laziness and put all my energy together and then prepare myself for these occasions.

FIGURE 1

MAP OF EARLIEST MIGRATIONS OF MODERN HUMANS, BEGINNING IN AFRICA BETWEEN 100,000 AND 50,000 YEARS AGO, CONTINUING INTO ASIA AND TO THE OTHER CONTINENTS, WITH APPROXIMATE DATES SUGGESTED BY THE ARCHEOLOGICAL RECORD.

Reproduced from Luigi Luca Cavalli-Sforza, *Genes, Peoples, and Languages* (London: Allen Lane and The Penguin Press, 2000), p. 94.

most fruitful of areas but, nonetheless, a region that could be used for hunting and gathering activities and also for agricultural purposes.

The next break of the population is the breakoff to Europe, which Cavalli-Sforza dates around 40,000–43,000 years ago, and the latest split-off is the one to America, across the Bering Strait, for which again, only very rough estimates exist; they range from 15,000 years to 50,000 years ago. And the spreading of the population on the American continent is estimated to have lasted about 1,000 years, from the North, all the way down to Patagonia, which would be something like eight miles per year, so not a large distance per year.

The spreading, at this time, is either by foot or, when that was significantly faster, by boat. Boat travel remained the fastest way of traveling until the domestication of horses, which occurs only some 6,000 years ago. Until that time, nothing but walking was possible, and as a matter of fact, as you probably know from your history lessons, that was pretty much the only way of transportation that existed on the American continent until the arrival of the Europeans. We always picture these Indians on horses, but of course, there existed no horses whatsoever and there existed actually, on the American continent, not even wheels. That is to say, people transported things by schlepping some wooden planks behind them, on which they had whatever they had to transport.

During these early times, until about 10,000 to 12,000 years ago, all of these populations, all of these people were hunters and gatherers, moving around at low speeds, mostly in small bands of 50–60 people, but several bands usually had some sort of connection. There exist biological reasons why minimal group sizes have to be about 500 people in order to prevent some sort of genetic degeneration, so one can expect that even if they were in small bands, that there was some sort of communication and intermarriage and so forth, with people of this group size.

The density of population was, as you can imagine, extremely low. The estimation is that in hunter-gatherer societies, you can have only one person per square mile. For more, for a larger population, the Earth did not produce enough foodstuff to support it. The population growth was extremely slow, partly because of birth control techniques used by people, by long breastfeeding, and things of that nature, and of course, because of high mortality rates. The estimation is that 100,000 years ago, at the beginning of this process that I'm talking about, the population size was about 50,000 in the world; 50,000 on the entire globe.

And 10,000 years ago, that is a period I will talk about a little bit later, the so-called Neolithic Revolution, when people began to settle down and begin agricultural existence, the numbers there are between 1 and 15 million and the estimation that most people accept is about 5 million. So, from 100,000 years to 10,000 years ago, 90,000 years of time, the population increases only from 50,000 to 5 million, and that is roughly a doubling of the population every 13,000–14,000 years.

To give you some sort of ballpark figure what the speed of population doubling is now, from the 1950s on, populations doubled every 35 years. So, you can see, based on this figure, what extremely small growth of population took place during this period. The groups, basically, simply broke away from each other, as I said, many times by boat, frequently also by foot. There existed then, for a considerable amount of time, 90,000 years or so, very little communication and intermingling between these breakaway groups, which explains the fact that quite different genetic stocks of people developed, because very limited interbreeding took place. In addition, there were the glacial periods, which cut off, sometimes for 10,000 or so years, communication between groups that were not far apart from each other distance-wise. The Alps, for instance, became essentially impassable, so people who were in the north lost all contact with people who were in the south.

Then there is the weather: the rains in Eurasia come mostly from the west, going eastward, so most of the snow accumulated in the west and the drier climates were in the east. People moved from the west to the east and then partially after the glacial periods were over returned back to more western regions. So, practically no contact between these groups. Of course, this is particularly pronounced in cases such as Australia and Borneo, which then became separated by large bodies of water, as compared to the periods when you could easily cross these straits. And there exists a general law, which is easy to grasp, that genetic distance increases in correlation with physical distance and with the separation in time.

I provided you with two charts that give you some rough indication of this. I have no intention of going into that in great detail, but Figure 2 is a tree diagram, which indicates roughly the distance in the genetic material of the populations living in these major areas and reflects in a way the breaking, the periods when populations broke away from each other. It indicates, for instance, that the first split occurred between Africa and Asia and then the second split occurred between Asia and Europe and the third one was Asia and America, and it indicates also the wide genetic distance, so to speak, between Africa, on the one hand, and the Oceanic population, on the other.

FIGURE 2

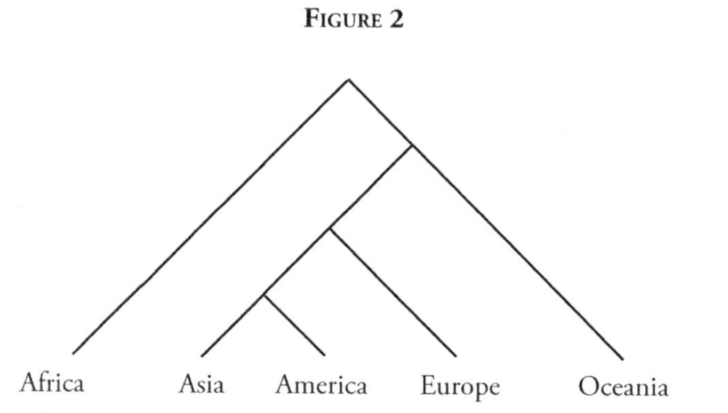

Reproduced from Luigi Luca Cavalli-Sforza, *Genes, Peoples, and Languages* (London: Allen Lane and The Penguin Press, 2000), p. 39.

Figure 3 is more detailed, as you see: it has on the left side the genetic relationships, how far or close some of the major ethnic groups are genetically, and on the right side, how close or distant they are in terms of their languages. There's obviously some sort of correlation between the genetic groups and the linguistic groups, but by no means a perfect one, which can be explained mostly by invasions by various people, who then spread their own language also in regions that were originally genetically different. Or sometimes you have regions that are genetically quite close, but they have brought languages from far away distances. An example would be, for instance, in the European scenery, the Finns and the Hungarians and the Turks, which have somewhat closely related languages, even though they are physically quite far removed from each other. I'll come back to this type of topic about

Figure 3
The Comparison of Genetic and Linguistic Trees

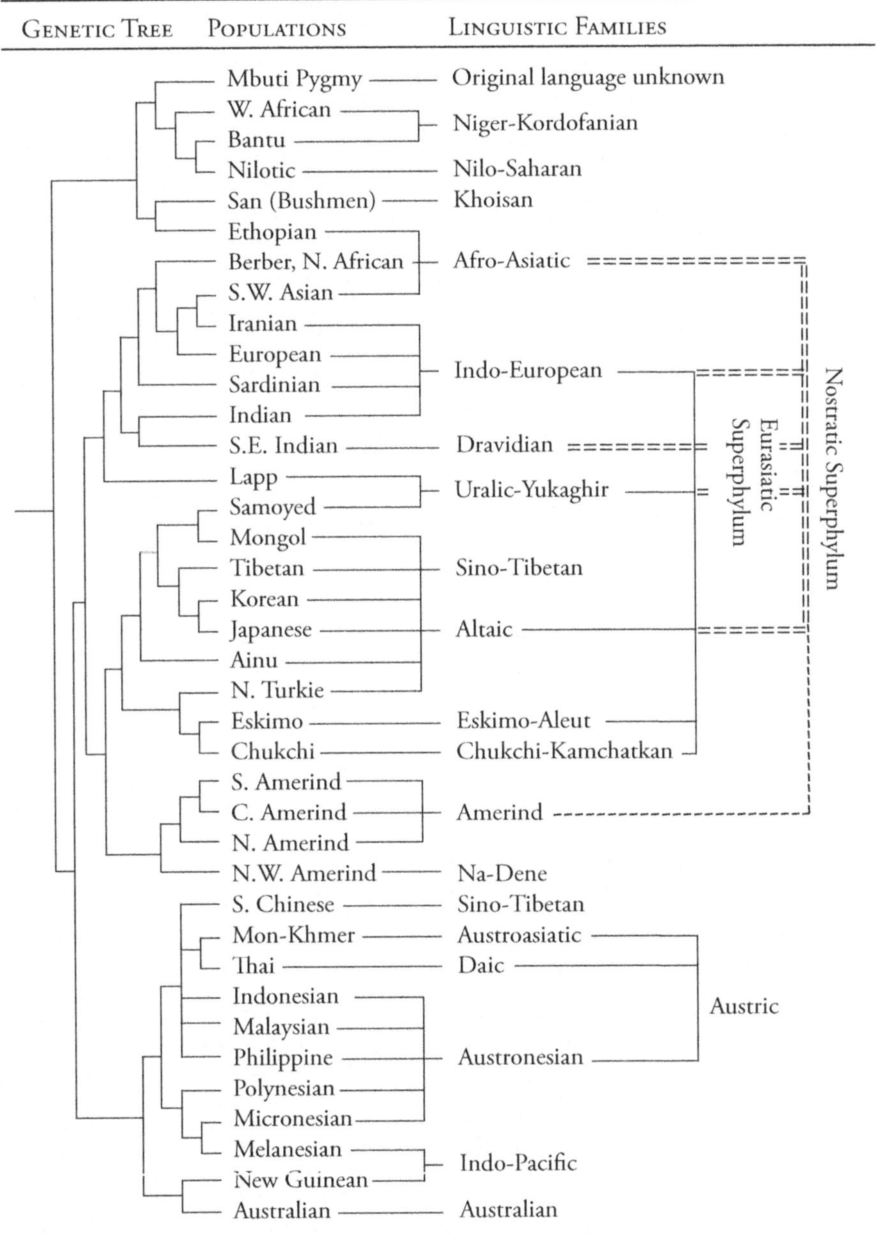

Reproduced from Luigi Luca Cavalli-Sforza, A. Piazza, P. Menozzi, and J.L. Mountain, "Reconstruction of Human Evolution: Bringing Together Genetic, Archeological, and Linguistic Data," *Proceedings of the National Academy of Science* 85 (1988): 6002–06.

different ethnicities and related subjects in a later lecture. For the current purpose, this is entirely sufficient, just to get some sort of feeling for how the separation and the movement of hunter-gatherers, with very little contact with each other, automatically brings these results about.

This separation and very limited cooperation between different groups, brings also about, a tendency to create a large variety of languages. You will see, later on, there exists, of course, also a tendency for languages to be reduced in number, when the contact between various groups becomes intensified. That is, when the division of labor is no longer restricted to these small groups, but becomes more extensive and more intensive, including ever larger regions of the population, then there is a countervailing tendency because then there exists, of course, a need for people to communicate with each other, and one can recognize that it is an advantage to speak languages that are spoken by very many people. If you are living more or less enclosed in small groups and the division of labor is restricted to these small groups, then there is no disadvantage to just having a different language for each one of these groups.

Currently, there exist about 5,000 to 6,000 languages. To give you an extreme example, 1,000 of these 5,000–6,000 languages are spoken in Guinea, and half of these 1,000 languages have no more than 500 speakers. That is pretty close to the number that I gave you for what the minimum size of a group has to be in order to avoid negative genetic effects. There are only a few languages in Guinea that are spoken by more than 100,000 people. This also tells us something about the state of development of this place that obviously, that is not a place in which the division of labor is very extensive and intensive. They are still living rather isolated and have only a division of labor within their little tribes, without much need to learn other languages, or for one language to take over other languages and become the dominant one. The division of labor, at this stage, is of a very, very limited kind—obviously, women tend to be more the gatherers; men tend to be more the hunters. There are some people who make tools, but the number of tools and instruments is also very limited. So, by and large, very small numbers of different professions, if we can talk about that at all; there is probably no one who is really specializing full time in certain types of activities.

The division of labor even shrinks at times during this period, which leads to a situation where people unlearn things that were already part of the accumulated knowledge of mankind. Those things took place, in particular, in the cases of New Guinea and Australia and Tasmania, places that for tens of thousands of years were completely isolated from anybody else and could not even occasionally adopt techniques or knowledge that had been accumulated in other parts of the world. For instance, the Australian Aborigines still used stone tools around the year 1800 in Tasmania, which was cut off for some 10,000 years from any other place; these people must obviously have known, at some point in time, the technique for constructing boats, but when they were rediscovered, they were not able to make boats. They must, at some time, have had the capability of using bows and arrows, but when they were rediscovered, they were not able to use arrows and bows because the population had become too small and no influx of innovation came in, so these people with the smaller populations simply became less informed and less knowledgeable than they must have been at the beginning. The same is also true, by the way, for Eskimos and Polynesians. The Polynesians also had partially unlearned the ability to make boats, even though they must have had this ability at some point in the past—unless they were very good swimmers.

As a little side remark, there is an explanation for why Polynesians tend to be a very fat people, namely that fat people had a survival advantage on long boat trips where they didn't know where they would end up. So, people who had accumulated a lot of body fat had a higher chance of finally finding the Fiji Islands or wherever they landed, which is an explanation why we still find massive, massive people in these places, far more massive than you find in other regions of the world.

We now arrive at one of the great revolutions in human development and that is a so-called Neolithic Revolution, which took place about 10,000–12,000 years ago. The main explanatory factor for this was that land became gradually scarcer and scarcer and more valuable, and pressure arose to find a solution to the problem of how to feed the people who could not walk around and break away and find new hunting and gathering places. They had to make it possible for people to live in larger numbers on smaller territories. Before, land was more or less treated as a free good, and if it is treated as a free good, there exists of course no incentive to appropriate it, to establish property in the land.

In the previous lecture, I explained that it was perfectly natural that people considered *their* bow and arrow to be *their* bow and arrow and the axe they carried to be *their* axe and so forth, and when they hunted buffalo, if I had hunted one down, then, of course, that became *my* buffalo. But property in land is a relatively new invention, so to speak, and the explanation is that land, all of a sudden, is perceived to be scarce. And as soon as it comes to be perceived as scarce, there will be attempts made by people to fence pieces off from other pieces, to mark places off from other places and claim them as mine or yours. The places where agriculture starts are naturally those places that have, by nature, an abundance of suitable plants; that is, where you have wild corn and wild wheat and wild rye, etc., people settle there and then begin to cultivate existing plants so as to breed better products. These are the places that we describe as the Fertile Crescent, what is today the Middle East around Iraq and Syria, on the one hand, and on the other hand, China, that is, places that are located close to rivers, and then later on, of course, also Egypt.

Figure 4 deals with examples of domesticated plants and animals by the date of earliest domestication and by region. This begins at about 8,000 BC. The only animal that had been domesticated before then was the dog, which you find on the opposite page. Dogs, of course, had been already of some use for hunters and gatherers. All the other animals are typical animals that are useful only in agricultural societies and not so much useful if you lead a hunter and gatherer lifestyle.

The thing that I would like to make you aware of here is, the remarkable observation that there existed, basically, no large-scale domesticated animals on the American continent, except for the llama, which is not exactly comparable in its versatility to horses and cows. There exists some explanations that Jared Diamond in *Guns, Germs, and Steel,* proposes, which don't sound too plausible to me. He is some sort of environmentalist. He explains, for instance, the fact that there are no large-scale domesticated animals on the American continent, by claiming that initially, there existed all the animals on the American continent that existed in Asia and Europe also, but on the American continent, overhunting took place. And then you ask, of course, "Why

FIGURE 4
EXAMPLES OF SPECIES DOMESTICATED IN EACH AREA

Area	*Domesticated*		*Earliest Attested Date of Domestication*
	Plants	*Animals*	
Independent Origins of Domestication			
1. Southwest Asia	wheat, pea, olive	sheep, goat	8500 B.C.
2. China	rice, millet	pig, silkworm	by 7500 B.C.
3. Mesoamerica	corn, beans, squash	turkey	by 3500 B.C.
4. Andes and Amazonia	potato, manioc	llama, guinea pig	by 3500 B.C.
5. Eastern United States	sunflower, goosefoot	none	2500 B.C.
? 6. Sahel	sorghum, African rice	guinea fowl	by 5000 B.C.
? 7. Tropical West Africa	African yams, oil palm	none	by 3000 B.C.
? 8. Ethiopia	coffee, teff	none	?
? 9. New Guinea	sugar cane, banana	none	7000 B.C.?
Local Domestication Following Arrival of Founder Crops from Elsewhere			
10. Western Europe	poppy, oat	none	6000–3500 B.C.
11. Indus Valley	sesame, eggplant	humped cattle	7000 B.C.
12. Egypt	sycamore fig, chufa	donkey, cat	6000 B.C.

Reproduced from Jared Diamond, *Guns, Germs, and Steel: The Fates of Human Societies* (New York: W.W. Norton, 1998), p.100.

did overhunting take place, why did they wipe out all of these animals and did not recognize in time the value of some of them, the potential to be domesticated, as compared to what people did in Eurasia?" And his explanation is that people arrived in America at a later date than in Asia and in Europe and at that date, the weapons technology was already further developed, so the killing potential was greater for those people active on the American continent, such that the extinction of animals resulted there and did not result in Eurasia. There exist, of course, also other explanations for this, to which I will come back in some future lecture. It might have also something to do, of course, with the lack of foresight, that there was more foresight among some people in Eurasia and less foresight in America, to prevent this sort of environmental catastrophe, as we might call it, from occurring.

Now, agricultural life allows a far greater density of population than a hunter-gatherer existence. As a matter of fact, it is estimated that 10 to 100 times as many people can live on the same piece of land if they engage in agriculture rather than in hunting and gathering activities. And we also recognize that as soon as you have settled down and built agricultural communities, then for the first time it becomes possible for capital to be accumulated. Imagine hunters and gatherers who just schlep around from place to place, there is only so many things that you can take with you. After all, you have to carry everything and most of the stuff becomes excess baggage. Now that you settle, of course, you can establish storage and you can accumulate things for bad seasons, and you can feed not only larger numbers, you can also turn your activity from one type of farming to other types of farming, from growing one type of cereal to growing other types of cereal and so forth.

Anthropologists compare the way of life of the hunters and gatherers to the way of life of the settlers; the agricultural people settled and, they point out, the life of hunters and gatherers was, in a way, easier, nicer. They spent only a few hours a day just hunting away and then they were lazing around, whereas the agricultural people worked for long periods of time, especially since this whole thing started in the Middle East, with comparatively nice weather all year around, and you could work also all year around, whereas hunters and gatherers had entire seasons off. So, anthropologists report, for instance, that the hunters and gatherers frequently laughed at the stupid agricultural settlers there, that they worked so hard and they themselves had such a nice and lazy life.

What is not true, however, which you find reported in some books, is that these hunter-gatherer societies turned out to be militarily superior over agricultural societies and regularly raided them. And if you think about it, while this is, of course, possible, there are compelling reasons why that should not be the case. That is why agricultural societies should have been, even in this area, that is, defending themselves, superior over hunter-gatherer societies, simply because they engage in capital accumulation, they have denser populations, they have far more men and more conflicts. Typically, it was not the hunter-gatherer societies that beat the agricultural societies, but vice versa.

Because of this, then, let me just say something about the population size again. With the Neolithic Revolution, so, from 10,000 to 12,000 years ago, the population doubles every 1,300 years, roughly, as compared with every 13,000 years prior to that. Again, these are all ballpark figures. In a later lecture, I will give you a table with some sort of population estimates. So, the estimation is that maybe 10,000 years ago, we had 5 million people at the beginning of the Neolithic Revolution, and in the year 1 AD, the numbers that are given, go from 170 million to 400 million. So, if you take the average of those estimates, then you come up with this rough idea of 1,300 years per doubling of the population. Now, this superiority of agricultural societies over hunter-gatherer societies is then responsible for the gradual spreading of these societies. This did not start at every place; it started at a few places, as I said, for the Fertile Crescent and some places in China, and gradually, the farmers take over more and more land.

The hunter-gatherers are first transformed into *herders*, because they don't roam around anymore; they have to deal with tamed animals, but the tamed animals, of course, are on the outskirts and even the herders gradually lose more and more land to the ever-expanding farming population. Again, if you just look at the current world, hunters and gatherers practically exist no more at all, except at the very fringes of the globe. And even herders exist only in very small places, again, far removed, in Siberia and Lapland and places of that kind. The superior civilization, if we want to use this term, the agricultural civilization, gradually expands outward. The time, for instance, when various plants and so forth appear in various regions, it takes about 5,000 years for agriculture to spread from the Fertile Crescent and to reach a place like England. So, that would be an expansion of something like slightly more than one kilometer per year, which is added to agriculturally used territory and taken away from hunter-gatherer territories.

The division of labor now intensifies, of course, quite a bit. There are not just three or four different types of occupations that you can do; with small villages coming into existence, craftsmen who are specialized in these tasks evolve far more specialization. There is also a certain amount of interregional trade now developing, whereas between the hunter-gatherer societies, as I said, there was practically no trading going on whatsoever, and of course innovations now spread in some sort of regular and permanent way. Again, hunter-gatherer societies are living side by side. It happens, but it happens more or less by accident that one group picks up a new technique that has been developed by another one. Now, in agricultural societies, people live next door to each other, being integrated, to a certain extent. And, through the division of labor, the diffusion of knowledge also takes place. That is, something that is developed in one place, will arrive eventually at some other place and will be imitated there, if it happens to be useful at those places. And of course the direction is always from the centers of civilization, i.e. the Fertile Crescent and the river valleys in China, to the periphery, where the wild people still live. And no longer does it take place that the division of labor breaks down as easily, that something is simply forgotten. As long as there is contact and the population size increases, the specialization progresses and innovations are transported from place to place.

And what I pointed out before: now, with agriculture, we see also that this previous tendency of languages to break up into larger and larger numbers of different languages does come to a certain halt. There is now more communication between them; there is a greater advantage to speaking languages that are spoken by many people and also, for the first time, a tendency to learn the languages of neighboring regions, because you trade and associate with them, to a certain extent, which you did not do during the previous phase of mankind.

Let me end this lecture by providing you with two quotes from Mises, the first one a quote the full implication of which will only become clear in the next lecture. Mises tries to explain why there is an inherent tendency in human development of extending the division of labor, of having more and more people participate in the division of labor and to intensify the division of labor, that is, to specialize more and more and dedicate your entire time to specific tasks, rather than to one hour this and another hour that, etc. And the second quote, which, again, leads over to the next lecture, is a quote where he describes the inherent limitations that purely agricultural societies have, which lets us expect that a new invention has to be made; again, just as we invented agriculture to solve the problem of increasing scarcity of land, mankind has to solve another challenge that is inherent in purely agricultural societies—that is, to develop industrial societies with cities in order to deal with the fact that, even in agricultural societies, we will again eventually reach the point when the land cannot support a steadily growing population—and a new institution allowing us to live on far denser, far smaller territories comes into being.

The first quote, as I said, deals with the cause of social evolution. Mises says,

> The simplest way to depict the evolution of society, is to show the distinction between two evolutionary tendencies, which are related to each other in the same way as intention and extension. Society develops subjectively and objectively. Subjectively, by enlarging its membership.[2]

We have seen how that takes place, reaching several million people at the beginning of the Neolithic Revolution and then shooting up from there at a more rapid rate.

> [S]ubjectively, by enlarging its membership and objectively, by enlarging the aims of its activities. Far more activities become possible in an agricultural society. We build huts; we build tools for which there was no need before; we build storage facilities, and so forth, enlarging the aims of human activities. Originally confined to the narrowest circles of people, to immediate neighbors, the division of labor gradually becomes more general until eventually, it includes all mankind. This process, still far from complete and never, at any point in history, completed, is finite. We can, of course,

[2]Ludwig von Mises, *Socialism: An Economic and Sociological Analysis* (1951; Auburn, Ala.: Ludwig von Mises Institute, 2009), p. 314.

> imagine a point when this process has reached an end, when all men on Earth form a unitary system of division of labor, it will have reached its goal. Side-by-side with this extension of the social bonds, goes a process of intensification. Social action embraces more and more aims and the area in which the individual provides for his own consumption becomes constantly narrower. We need not pause at this stage to ask, whether this process will eventually result in the specialization of all productive activity, but again, the tendency is clearly in this direction.[3]

And now, an interesting quote on what I might call, the limitations of purely agricultural societies. Mises says,

> We may depict conditions of a society of agriculturalists, in which every member tills a piece of land large enough to provide himself and his family with the indispensable necessities of life. We may include, in such a picture, the existence of a few specialists, artisans like smiths and professional men like doctors. We might even go further and assume that some men do not own a farm, but work as laborers on other people's farms. The employer remunerates them for their help and takes care of them when sickness or old age disables him.
>
> This scheme of an ideal society, was at the bottom of many utopian plans. It was by and large, realized for some time in some communities. The nearest approach to its realization was probably the commonwealth which the Jesuit padres established in the country which is today Paraguay. There is, however, no need to examine the merits of such a system of social organization. Historical evolution burst it asunder. Its frame was too narrow for the number of people who are living today on the Earth's surface.

---

[3]Ibid.

> The inherent weakness of such a society is, that the increase in population must result in progressive poverty. If the estate of a deceased farmer is divided among its children, the holdings finally become so small that they can no longer provide sufficient sustenance for a family. Everybody is a land owner, but everybody is extremely poor. Conditions, as they prevailed in large areas of China, provide a sad illustration of the misery of the tillers of small parcels. The alternative to this outcome is the emergence of the huge mass of landless proletariats. Then, a wide gap separates the disinherited paupers from the fortunate farmers. They are a class of pariahs whose very existence presents society with an insoluble problem. They searched in vain for a livelihood; society has no use for them. They are destitute.[4]

And here, then, a solution to another problem has to be developed, and that is the solution of industrial capitalism—the development of towns and money—which allows another push in the growth of mankind and in the specialization of tasks, and I will talk about that in the next lecture.

[4]Ludwig von Mises, *Human Action: A Treatise on Economics*, scholar's edition (1949; Auburn, Ala.: Ludwig von Mises Institute, 1998), p. 831.

LECTURE 3

Money and Monetary Integration: The Growth of Cities and the Globalization of Trade

---

I WANT TO CONTINUE THE story from yesterday about the division of labor. So far, I have presented more or less a historical tale, and now I want to add a few theoretical considerations about why there is division of labor, and then from there continue on to the development of money, which intensifies the division of labor still further. We will also discuss the role of cities and city growth, and that will be continued in the lecture this afternoon on capital and capital accumulation.

I mentioned already yesterday that the fact of humans speaking to each other, arguing with each other, using language, indicates their social nature. Something else should be mentioned in this connection, and that is that at the beginning of mankind, it is difficult to imagine only two grown-up people being faced with the question, "Should we cooperate or not cooperate?," when keeping in mind also that there are different generations of people alive, which automatically makes it easier to understand why there is cooperation. Obviously, the older generation pressures the younger one to adopt certain standards and finds some advantages in the division of labor, but be that as it may, I want now to develop the case of the division of labor as Ludwig von Mises presents it, that is, assuming that there are grown-up adults, and that there is no language in existence initially.

Can we still, somehow, explain why people do not remain in self-sufficient isolation, but begin dividing their labor up and engage in exchanges based on the division of labor? In order to understand this, let's first assume that all individuals are perfectly identical to each other, perfect clones of each other, and that also land, that is, those things that we find in front of us as nature-given resources, are perfectly identical for every individual. What would then occur? That is a relatively easy prediction that we can make. If we assume that all people have the same desires, the same knowledge, and the same external equipment, then the result would be that every person will produce the same sort of things in the same quantities and in the same qualities—and in such a situation, it is obvious that there's simply no room for any type of exchange. What should I exchange if everybody has exactly the same things and uses up these things in exactly the same pattern as everybody else does, which simply follows from the assumptions that we have made, of perfect identity of labor and land. The first recognition, then, is that if it were not for the fact of differences with regard to land and/or labor, not even the idea of division of labor (and, based on the division of labor, exchange) would ever enter any person's mind.

Even if there are differences between labor, ourselves and man, it is not necessary that people divide their labor and exchange based on division of labor. They could still decide that "I will produce everything on my own and remain self-sufficient while in isolation." Mises makes the point that psychologists and sociologists frequently explain the rise of the division of labor by assuming some sort of instinct to truck and barter. You'll find this, for instance, in Adam Smith. He explains it by an instinct: humans are instinctively drawn to each other and to truck and barter with each other. Mises, however, points out something very interesting, that is to say, we don't need to make this assumption. We can make the assumption that actually every person hates everybody else and still explain how a division of labor can emerge. And obviously, explanations that require less in terms of assumptions are better than explanations that require us to make all sorts of assumptions in order to come up with our conclusion.

Let's assume everybody hates each other. Why would people nonetheless engage in the division of labor? Mises simply points out that the division of labor will arise as long as every person prefers more goods over fewer goods, as long as every person is perfectly selfish and wants to have more rather than less. This is entirely sufficient in order to explain why they do not remain in self-sufficient isolation. There are, as you might have heard in your microeconomics classes, two reasons for this.

The first one is called the *absolute* advantage of division of labor, which refers to a situation where one person is particularly good at doing one thing and another person is particularly good at doing something else. The reason for this can be internal, that he personally has talents that somebody else does not have and somebody else has talents that the other person does not have, or it can be due to the fact that one person lives on the mountainside and has certain opportunities that somebody who lives on the seaside does not have, or it can be a combination of these two factors, that is, differences of land and in labor. And given the fact that time is scarce, it is immediately clear that an advantage would result if each person specializes in those things in which he is particularly good, because then the total amount of goods that will be produced will be larger than it would be if both individuals were to decide to produce all goods, both goods, on our own and to not engage in the division of labor.

The second reason was first discussed by David Ricardo. Ricardo, however, applied this argument to different nations, and the advantage of Mises's presentation of this argument is to show that it applies, strictly speaking, also, to the individual level. That is the so-called *comparative* advantage of the division of labor, which refers to the conceivably worst-case scenario where one person is all-around superior. At every production process, he is more efficient than the other person, and the other person is all-around inferior as far as his productive capabilities are concerned. And the question is then, "Does it make sense for those types of individuals, one all-around superior, one all-around inferior, to engage in a division of labor?" And without going into great detail and trying to prove this sort of thing, it is entirely sufficient to make an intuitive case for the answer: yes, even under those circumstances, division of labor is beneficial, provided that these two individuals divide their labor up in the following way. The person who is all-around superior chooses to specialize in those things in which he has a particularly great advantage, and the person who is all-around inferior specializes in that area in which his disadvantage is comparatively small. Let's take an example: a surgeon and a gardener. Among the two, the surgeon is the superior surgeon and he is also a superior gardener—and because his time is scarce, it is advantageous for him to specialize in that activity where his advantage is particularly great, namely in the area of surgery, leaving the activity of gardening to the other person, despite the fact that the surgeon would also be a better gardener than the gardener is. But given the fact that his advantage is greater in one area than in the other and that time spent on one activity can no longer be spent on another activity, dividing their labor in this way and then, based on this division of labor, engaging in exchanges, the standard of living of both individuals will be higher.

Let me quote Mises to this effect, that is, explaining why it is that we don't find people who remain in self-sufficient isolation. There might be a few people who try it, but even they do not completely do it. In the old days of the hippie movement, there were, of course, some people who tried to live off the earth, as you might remember, but even they did not live directly off the earth. They drove their campers up the mountain and led the primitive life there, but as soon as they ran out of gas, they didn't drill for oil on the top of the mountain, but went on down to the next Shell station and got a refill. If they would not have done that, we never would have heard anything from these people again. So, Mises says,

> If and as far as labor under the division of labor is more productive than isolated labor, and if and as far as man is able to realize this fact, human action itself tends toward cooperation and association; man becomes a social being, not in sacrificing his own concerns for the sake of a mythical Moloch, society, but in aiming at an improvement in his own welfare. Experience teaches that this condition—higher productivity achieved under division of labor—is present because its cause—

> the inborn inequality of men and the inequality in the geographical distribution of the natural forces of production—is real. Thus we are in a position to comprehend the course of social evolution.[1]

And now to a very important insight that Mises derives from this—again, recall, I pointed out that contrary to people like Adam Smith, for instance, who stipulated some inborn sympathy among mankind as the ultimate cause of division of labor, Mises reverses this argument and says, "It is precisely the higher productivity of the division of labor which makes us dependent on each other, based on our recognition that we all benefit from this dependency on others that we then develop sympathetic feelings toward others." So, it is not the sympathy that explains division of labor; it is the selfish motivation to begin the division of labor, that then, as a result of the division of labor, lets feelings of sympathy among mankind develop. So, sympathy results from, but is not the cause of, the division of labor. And again, a very interesting quote to this effect. Mises says,

> [T]here can emerge between members of society feelings of sympathy and friendship and a sense of belonging together. These feelings are the source of man's most delightful and most sublime experiences. They are the most precious adornment of life; they lift the animal species man to the heights of a really human existence. However, they are not, as some have asserted, the agents that have brought about social relationships. They are the fruits of social cooperation, they thrive only within its frame; they did not precede the establishment of social relations and are not the seed from which they spring.[2]

And then he elaborates a little bit more on this. He says,

---

[1]Ludwig von Mises, *Human Action: A Treatise on Economics*, scholar's ed. (1949; Auburn, Ala.: Ludwig von Mises Institute, 1998), p. 160.

[2]Ibid., p. 144.

> The mutual sexual attraction of male and female is inherent in man's animal nature and independent of any thinking and theorizing. It is permissible to call it original, vegetative, instinctive, or mysterious....However, neither cohabitation, nor what precedes it and what follows, generates social cooperation and societal modes of life. The animals too join together in mating, but they have not developed social relations. Family life is not merely a product of sexual intercourse. It is by no means natural and necessary that parents and children live together in the way in which they do in the family. The mating relation need not result in family organization. The human family is an outcome of thinking, planning, and acting. It is this very fact which distinguishes it radically from those animal groups which we call *per analogiam* animal families.[3]

So again, it is the recognition of the advantages of division of labor that makes stable family relationships, rather than people breaking up and going their own way.

Now, the division of labor then, because it is more productive, allows also, as I already indicated yesterday in my lecture, for population growth that otherwise would not be possible. The easiest way to convince ourselves of this is to engage in a thought experiment, what would happen to the world population if we were to decide from now on to withdraw from all social interaction and become self-sufficient producers. As I already intimated with that hippie example, it can be easily seen that if we were to do something like this, most of mankind would be wiped out within a few days because we would not be able to provide ourselves with all the amenities that we have gotten used to. As soon as our truck wears out, we wouldn't be able to fix it; as soon as our milk runs out, well, in my case, more importantly, as soon as my beer runs out, I would be in deep trouble.

Note that the division of labor also allows the so-called unfit to survive. But it is precisely these people, who under very primitive conditions,

---

[3]Ibid., p. 167.

due to some deficiencies of their bodily functions or sensory functions, would be condemned to starve and die, who can survive and lead productive lives and even become rich and wealthy individuals as a result of the division of labor. As a result of all this, as I explained, we first have agricultural societies developing. These agricultural societies have a minimal amount of division of labor; they are still, to a large extent, self-sufficient. But then, as Mises described in the quote that I gave you yesterday, problems arise if the population increases: the plots become smaller and smaller; land becomes more and more valuable, and we have to find a solution to this growing mass of population. And the solution is a deepening and intensifying of the division of labor, which leads to the formation, out of small villages, of cities, where we have specialized professions developing that provide the countryside with specialized tools and receive from the countryside the foodstuff necessary to lead their city life.

With city life also comes for the first time (due to the fact that city life already indicates a larger amount of capital accumulation, and leads to a situation where people reach a certain level of wealth, have a certain amount of leisure time) the development of science or the first attempts toward science, which requires leisure time to reflect about natural laws, and so forth, and also very importantly, the development of a written language, which again constitutes a great advance in human development above and beyond the development of a language itself—because in this way, we are no longer dependent on oral tradition, one generation telling the following generation what to do, what they have learned and so forth, but we now have the ability to just freeze and make permanent experiences that were collected by previous generations. It also becomes far easier to transport this information to far and distant places, far more easy than would be possible if we had to rely on oral traditions. Written languages developed first around 5,000 years ago, and we do know that some regions on the globe never reached this stage of development of having a written language. Some places only received written languages once they were rediscovered by Europeans. There existed no written language on the African continent, and only very small attempts in some small regions on the American continent, of written languages.

I mentioned Carroll Quigley yesterday in connection with his claim that one of the marks of civilizations is that, civilizations no longer live the parasitic life, but are societies that add something to the existing resources. Quigley gives, apart from this, a few other characteristics that he considers to be constitutive of civilization, and those are societies that have cities that have progressed beyond the village level and that possess a written language. The first civilization or first society that fulfills this requirement of a civilization, in Quigley's sense, would be those societies that developed in the Fertile Crescent, today's Iraq and Syria.

Let me just give you some ballpark figures about the size of the cities that came into being during this period 4,000–6,000 years ago. The biggest city for many centuries was Uruk, the remnants of which are in Iraq. Around 3700 BC, Uruk as the first city had a population of about 14,000 people. So, by our standards, it was merely a large village but at that time, obviously, a major breakthrough as compared to village sizes. And this city, Uruk, in the next 1,000 years or so, by 2800 BC, grew to a population size of 80,000 people. This is already a significant size, in which one can imagine that such a size city must display quite a significant amount of division of labor within the nonagricultural field. So, that was 80,000 people in 2800 BC. After that, the city of Uruk declines. Other cities take its place as the dominant city.

The next one is Akkad, which is also in the same region, which reaches the size of 60,000 inhabitants. Then the biggest cities appear in Egypt: Memphis and Thebes and Avaris. The biggest size of towns during this period of the Babylonian and Egyptian civilizations, was about 100,000. If we go to more recent periods, there is a time, let's say, during the Roman Empire, when we find cities already of a significantly larger size. Rome itself, at its peak, had a population of about a million people, and we will see later on that there is also economic disintegration: a city that had a million inhabitants at one time shrinks, a few hundred years later, to a size of 20,000.

There are periods—and I'll come back to that in more detail—in which you can see there is faster population growth, more intensive division of labor, greater population growth, wider specialization and so forth, but there are also periods in which this sort of thing gets destroyed and populations shrink, the division of labor shrinks, population size in cities goes down and so forth. Athens, at the peak of its development, had about 250,000 inhabitants, and one of the premier harbors and trading centers during this time, Alexandria, had a population of about 400,000 people.

Now, with cities also come merchants and money. I would like to add that to Quigley's definition of developed civilizations, as places that have cities and written language, as an additional criterion of developed civilizations, to point out that they must have a specialized merchant class, people who are engaged in small-distance and in particular, also long-distance trade and, of course, with long-distance trade, the development of money.

I will interrupt my historical considerations and give a brief explanation for the development of money. Just as we can rationally reconstruct why it is that people engage in the division of labor and why there is a tendency for the division of labor to become more extensive and more intensive, so we can also provide a rational reconstruction of the development of money as a solution to a problem that arises out of trade in a premonetary economy. If we have a barter economy, in which people trade consumer goods for other consumer goods or consumer goods for producer goods, and production takes place for exchange purposes, or at least partially for exchange purposes, rather than for self-sufficient supplies, then the problem automatically arises that sometimes I might have produced something for the purpose of exchanging it for something else, but the person who has what I want is not interested in my products, but wants something else.

Trade, in this situation, is only possible if we have what is called a double coincidence of wants, that is to say, I must have what you want and you must have what I want. If only one of these accidents occurs, I have what you want, but you don't have what I want, then, clearly, trading comes to a standstill, and in such a situation, people are obviously looking for some sort of solution to this halting of trade, given the fact that they produced for exchange purposes, and not for the purpose of using things themselves. And again, Mises, drawing on the writings of Carl Menger, has a very beautiful explanation for what the solution looks like to this problem. If you cannot trade directly, what will happen is—and we don't have to assume that this happens instantaneously or that every group of people makes the same discovery at the same time—we only have to assume that there are some brighter people in society who make the simple discovery that not all goods that are traded in barter are equally marketable. That is to say, not all goods traded in barter are equally frequently used by people. Some goods are used by more people on more occasions and other goods are used by fewer people on fewer occasions.

And in such a situation, where I cannot receive for my goods what I directly want, I can still gain an advantage, make myself better off, following only selfish instincts, if I succeed in surrendering my goods for something that is more marketable than my own goods are. If I receive something that is more marketable, even if I have no interest in using that as a consumer good or a producer good, the advantage that I gain is the advantage that a more marketable good can, of course, more easily be resold for those things that I really want. That is, I have a more marketable good in my hands which is of no direct use to me as a consumer or as a producer, but I have demanded it as what is called a *medium of exchange*, as a facilitator of exchange. It facilitates exchange because there are more people on more occasions who are willing to accept these goods than the goods I had initially offered for sale.

Then, the degree of marketability of this particular good increases even more so because now there are people who demand this good because they want to have it as a consumer good and a producer good as before and, in addition, there's one person who demands this good for a different motive, the motive being, I will use it as a medium of exchange, as a facilitator of exchange. And then it becomes easier for the next bright person in society to make the same discovery: whenever he gets into difficulties trading his good directly against those things that he wants, he makes the same move. All I have to do is find a good that is more marketable than my own and the likelihood that he picks the same has already increased, due to the fact that there was already one brighter guy before him.

And then we have, very quickly, a convergence toward one medium of exchange that is used in society all over the place, and we call this a common medium of exchange or *money*. Two advantages that arise as soon as we have a common medium of exchange in existence is that now, with a common medium of exchange in existence, we can sell and buy instantly without having to wait for double coincidences of wants to come into existence.

The second advantage that arises with the existence of a common medium of exchange is that now we can engage in *cost accounting*. After all, recall that we produce for sale on the market; we do not produce for our own use. If we produce for the market, then we want to make sure that those things that go into the production of certain products are less valuable than those things that we produce with our inputs. Or to put it differently, we want to make sure that our output is more valuable than our input. But in a barter economy the outputs and the inputs are in different units—they are incommensurable. However, as soon as all our inputs and our output sell against one common medium of exchange, we have a common denominator; we can now compare, or add up, all the inputs in terms of money and we can express our output in terms of money, and we can now determine whether we made *profits or losses*—profits indicating that we did indeed turn less valuable resources into more valuable resources, which is, after all, the purpose of production—or, if we made losses, this tells us that we wasted valuable resources in order to turn them into something that was less valuable than those things that were used in order to produce our product, which would give us a signal that we should discontinue this type of production process.

Now, as we imagine that the division of labor expands and ultimately reaches and encompasses the entire globe, as different regions begin to trade with each other, we can see that there will be in the market also a tendency for one type of regional money to outcompete other regional types of money, with the ultimate result to be expected being that there will be only one or, at the most, two types of money left over, which are used universally. That is to say, such a money, a money that is more widely used, more widely accepted, is obviously advantageous over a money that is only used in certain small regions. If we have different monies being used in certain small regions, then we are, strictly speaking, still in a system of partial barter. If I want to trade with a different region, I first have to find somebody who wants my money and is willing to give me his money, and only then can I proceed to make my purchases. If you have, however, only one money used on a worldwide scale, then it is obviously possible that without any necessity for double coincidences of wants, immediate trading can take place. These two tendencies, division of labor expanding and the tendency of money to become one universally used money, obviously reinforce each other and deepen and intensify the division of labor.

At this point, to emphasize this tendency for the globalization of trade facilitated by the universality of one money having outcompeted the initial different sorts of money—let me give an important quote from Mises, to which I will return at a later point again. Mises says,

> A social theory that was founded on Darwinism would either come to the point of declaring that war of all against all was the natural and necessary form of human intercourse, thus denying that any social bonds were possible; or, it would have, on the other hand, to show why peace does and must reign within certain groups and yet, on the other, to prove that the principle of peaceful union which leads to the formation of these associations is ineffective beyond the circle of the group, so that the groups among themselves must struggle.[4]

You notice that the argument here is that most people have very little difficulty accepting the thesis that yes, there are peaceful relationships between the inhabitants of village A and village B, or tribe A and tribe B, because everybody sees that that is, of course, taking place. If you accept the Darwinian explanation, this is already difficult to explain, but the next struggle, the next problem, the more decisive one, is that people who accept these Darwinian interpretations have to explain why there should be division of labor and peaceful relationships within a group but not between different groups. After all, the same principles seem to be at work. Mises then says this: "peaceful union, which leads to the formation of these associations, is ineffective beyond the circle of the group, so that the groups among themselves must struggle." And Mises then says,

---

[4]Ludwig von Mises, *Socialism: An Economic and Sociological Analysis*, trans. J. Kahane (1951; Auburn, Ala.: Ludwig von Mises Institute, 2009), p. 318.

> This is precisely the rock on which all non-liberal social theories founder. If one recognizes a principle which results in the union of all Germans, of all Dolichocephalians or all Proletarians and forms a special nation, race, or class out of these individuals, then this principle cannot be proved to be effective only *within* the collective groups. The anti-liberal social theories skim over the problem by confining themselves to the assumption that the solidarity of interests within the groups is so self-evident, as to be accepted without further discussion, and by taking pains only to prove the existence of the conflict of interests between groups and the necessity of conflict as the sole dynamic force of historical development. But if war is to be the father of all things, the fruitful source of historical progress, it is difficult to see why its fruitful activity should be restricted within states, nations, races and classes. If Nature needs war, why not the war of all against all, why merely the war of all groups against all groups?[5]

This is a very powerful description of, or explanation for, why the same principles that lead groups to cooperate peacefully are also operative at work when it comes to cooperation between different groups. The same reasons apply there as they apply within each group. The division of labor is beneficial, because it benefits all groups participating in it, just as it benefits all individuals within a group. And a development of money toward a universal medium of exchange is beneficial in the same way as the development of regional money is beneficial for the inhabitants of just a small region.

Now, back to a few historical remarks, illustrating this tendency of globalizing the division of labor and the development of a universal money integrating all regions, all classes, all societies. From very early on, after the development of cities and a merchant class and regional monies, we have the development of long-distance trade. We already have something that is called the Silk Road, connecting Asia to Europe

---

[5]Ibid.

via the Middle East, which is still sort of the center of civilization, at that time, some 4,000 years ago. That is, 4,000 years ago there already existed trading routes of thousands of kilometers connecting Europe with Asia, trading routes that are protected by either the merchants themselves or by those people who live nearby and have an interest that the trade takes place through their areas. There exists, during the Roman Empire—which at least in the ancient history provides examples for the deepest and widest economic integration—permanent contact around 200 BC between Rome and Han, China, where caravans of people move steadily and trade various goods back and forth. Very early on we also have regular sea travel; the Chinese regularly sent ships all the way to places such as India, for instance. And from the western part, there are regular sea trade routes from the Persian Gulf to India as well, especially after the discovery of the monsoon winds. That is, the monsoon winds, I forget exactly which direction, are such that for half a year they blow toward the east and for the other half of the year they blow to the west. So, once people discovered this regular pattern, relatively large-scale shipping operations could be conducted from the Persian Gulf to India and back.

Again, those sorts of things, just simply discovering how the wind blows, took quite some time; in some cases it was comparatively easy, as with the monsoon winds, where you have long periods blowing one way and long periods blowing the other way. It was far more difficult, for instance, to find the appropriate sea routes across the Atlantic, going in one direction and then coming back in the other direction, since you typically cannot take the same routes. And it was even more difficult for the Pacific, where the routes are very different for going one way and for going the other. Again, hundreds of years of experience were necessary in order to develop detailed knowledge about the most appropriate routes to take, and this only became a nonproblem with the development of steamships, which is, of course, a comparatively recent development.

This intensive long-distance trade is reflected in the fact that we can find Roman coins in places like South India, but Roman coins were not the most popular coins, because Roman coins suffered from frequent coin-clipping operations by various rulers. So, for some 800 years or so, from about 300 AD to the twelfth century, the most popular money was produced by Constantinople and the name of it was *solidus* or *bezant*, (obviously named after Bezant, or Byzantium), and they gained a reputation of being the most reliable, most honest coins, subject to practically no coin clipping or adding of less valuable metals to it. Trading markets, of course, prefer good money over bad money.

You might have heard about the so-called Gresham's law, which states that bad money drives out good money, but this law only holds if there are price controls in effect, only if the exchange ratios of different monies are fixed and no longer reflect the market forces. Is it the case that bad money drives out good money under normal circumstances without any interference? No, for money holds to exactly the same law that holds for every other good. Good goods drive out bad goods. Good money drives out bad money, so this bezant was for something like 800 years considered to be the best money available and was preferred by merchants from India to Rome to the Baltic Sea. In all of these regions, you can find this type of coin being used, and diggings have produced evidence of the use of these coins at these far distant places.

To continue the story, we have the discovery of America taking place. Those areas had been completely unknown to the Western Eurasian world before—it actually takes until about 1850 for the final explorations into the interior of Africa to take place, and we can say roughly that by the mid-nineteenth century the entire world had become known to mankind. And it is not an accident, then, that around this time what emerges is, for the first time, a clear-cut tendency for one or two commodity monies to outcompete everything else. That is, at the end of the nineteenth century, we have an international gold standard developing. For a while, there was competition between gold and silver. There were certain areas that preferred silver. For instance, before 1908, China and Persia and a few South American countries still used silver, but by 1900, the rest of the world was on a gold standard. This is precisely what one would predict based on economic theory, a tendency toward a one world commodity money coming into existence. Of course, there is always some sort of interference and messing up by governments in this process, and we have not talked about this yet. So far, the entire reconstruction that I give is a reconstruction of what would happen without any government interference. This problem of government interference will occupy us only in later lectures.

And then we can say that from 1914 on, while we have probably reached the most complete economic integration in human history, the most encompassing economic integration, most intensive division of labor, including the entire globe; from 1914 on, disintegration set in again. Most visibly, of course, documented by the fact that we currently no longer have an international commodity money; we have, instead, a large variety of national, freely fluctuating paper currencies that is a regression to a situation that we might consider to be partial barter again. That is something that we had already overcome in history, and we have gone back to a situation that we had already successfully solved. And you see, of course, currently, under a paper money regime, which requires, of course, the existence of governments—I have to jump ahead here for a moment at least. Under a paper money regime, you can see, however, the same tendency at work that you saw as a natural tendency with the commodity money, that is, trying to create a paper currency used worldwide, to bring such a thing into existence. We see the attempts of monetary integration in Europe, for instance, so that we currently have only three major currency blocks: the euro on the one hand, the dollar on the other, and the yen as the third one. All the other ones don't count for much, because very little trade is conducted in other currencies besides these. This might change one day, of course, with China opening up completely, but as you have certainly heard, there exist powerful international organizations that promote the idea of a one-world central bank, issuing a one-world paper currency. The argument that they use for this, the kernel of truth in their argument, is, of course, precisely the same one that I explained here. It is simply advantageous to have a single money, because trading becomes easier with just one money instead of a multitude of fluctuating moneys. The drawback in the current situation is, of course, that this one world paper money will be a money that will be produced and managed by a monopoly institution such as a world bank, and can be inflated at will. And we would likely see a larger amount of inflation with such an institution in place than we ever saw in world history before.

Allow me this little side remark. If you have paper money, then it is actually an advantage to have competing paper monies, because the inflationary desires of each individual central bank are curtailed by the noncooperation of other governments. If country A inflates their paper money more than country B, its currency will fall in the currency market and people will tend to drop this type of money and adopt monies that are more stable. If you have paper money, which is, in effect, as I said, sort of dysfunctional to the very purpose of money in the first place, and represents a regression in human development—if you have paper money in existence, then competing paper monies fluctuating against each other is an advantage over a worldwide produced paper money. But you can have a worldwide money also, one that is provided completely independent of governments, and that was precisely what we had at the end of the nineteenth century, namely an international gold standard, which could just as well be have been a silver standard. (Economic theory does not predict whether it will be gold or silver; economic theory only predicts that there will be a tendency toward one type of money being used on a worldwide scale because it is a function of money to be a facilitator of exchange, and, of course, we can recognize that a money that is used all over the place facilitates exchange more so than any other possible money that only exists in various smaller regions.)

LECTURE 4

Time Preference, Capital, Technology, and Economic Growth

THIS LECTURE WILL BE ON time preference, on interest and capital, and on capital accumulation. I have already to a certain extent touched upon the problem of capital accumulation. We said that agricultural societies made it possible for the first time for capital goods to be accumulated, whereas the possibilities for accumulating much in terms of capital goods in hunter-gatherer societies that move from place to place are very limited. And this subject is the third dimension that we need to cover in order to understand the wealth of nations, apart from ideological factors, which I will come to in a future lecture, besides the division of labor, the development of money, and the universalization of money. Capital accumulation is the third leg on which societies stand.

I will begin with some theoretical considerations, some theoretical explanations about the phenomenon of time preference and how it relates to capital and capital accumulation in particular. People do not just have a preference for more goods over less. I discussed how this preference explains, for instance, why there is a division of labor.

People also have a preference for goods earlier, satisfaction earlier, as compared to satisfaction later, goods later. Mankind cannot wait forever for satisfaction. Waiting for certain results involves a sacrifice, and without capital goods—recall, we make the distinction between consumer goods, which are directly useful, and producer goods, which are only indirectly useful. There are very few desires that we can satisfy immediately or instantaneously, well, maybe picking a berry, that immediately leads to satisfaction. And there is, of course, leisure time, just lazing around, that can also be immediately satisfied without doing anything else about it.

But, most of our desires require that we use intermediate products in order to satisfy them, or we need intermediate products in order to be more productive; that is, if you want to increase the amount of immediately usable consumer goods, we have to go about it in some sort of roundabout way, rather than picking berries and satisfying ourselves directly in this way. What capital goods do is they allow us a greater production of the same goods, or they allow us to produce goods that cannot be attained at all without the help of capital goods. And in order to attain capital goods, it is necessary that we save, that we consume less than we could consume, and use these saved-up funds to feed ourselves during the period of time that is necessary in order to complete the construction of capital goods, with the help of which, then, we can attain larger output of consumer goods or attain goals that we could not attain without capital goods at all.

This restriction on possible consumption is what we call *saving*, and the transfer of our saved funds, allocating—using—land and labor to construct or bring into existence capital goods, is called *investment*. And the question that we always face is the following. Does the utility that is achieved by the higher productivity of longer, roundabout production processes, that is, a utility that we achieve by roundabout methods of production, exceed the subjective sacrifice that we must make of present goods that we could conceivably consume? Or to put it differently, the decision of an actor regarding what objects to invest in will depend on the expected utility of the forthcoming consumer goods, on the durability of these forthcoming consumer goods, and on the length of time that it takes before we attain these future consumer goods. And we can then explain the entire act of deciding whether or not to perform an act of capital formation as the balancing of relative utilities—that's the expected present utility that we attach to future goods, as compared to the utility of present goods available through consumption, discounted by the rate of time preference. That is, by the rate at which we value present goods more highly than future goods. Present goods are always valued more highly than future goods; present goods sell at a premium against future goods—or to put it the other way around, future goods sell at a discount against present goods. And this phenomenon, this discount or this premium, depending on what the angle is from which we look at the phenomenon, is called *interest.*

I want to illustrate these initial abstract remarks by looking for a moment at a simple Robinson Crusoe economy. Let's assume that Robinson Crusoe is the most knowledgeable person on Earth. He knows all the technological recipes that mankind knows, but he is stranded alone on an island. On this island, there is initially nothing other than *land,* that is, nature-given resources, and *labor* from his own body, and his own *knowledge* incorporated in it. And let us assume that the immediately available consumer good that is available to him is fish, and thus he now has to make a decision as to how he will produce this consumer good of fish. Given, as I said, that Robinson Crusoe knows every technological recipe under the sun, we can imagine that he knows various techniques for how to attain his end, that is, fish as a consumer good. He can, for instance, use his bare hands to obtain fish, by grabbing into the water and pulling the fish out. He can build a net with which to catch fish. He can build a fishing trawler, a boat with a net to catch fish, and we might easily imagine that there exist various other technologies that he is aware of as well.

The question that Robinson Crusoe faces is then: "What shall I do, how shall I produce fish?" And the first thing that is worth pointing out here is that the fact that he knows about extremely productive methods of catching fish, let's say using a fishing trawler, that this fact does not help him much in his initial situation. And the reason for this should be obvious: the reason has to do with the fact that he is constrained by time preference; that is, he cannot wait forever for the satisfaction of his most urgent desires, and if he were to start building a fishing trawler then he would likely be long dead from starvation before the fishing trawler is ever completed. So, he will have to start in a capital-less mode of production, without any capital goods, just using his bare hands to get fish out of the pond or the river or the ocean. When he's done at the end of the day and he has caught ten fish, he will have to make a decision what to do with these ten fish.

Obviously, if he decides that he will consume all ten fish by the end of the day, then the following day he will be in the exact same position that he was on the day before. On the other hand, if he decides to put away some fish, a certain fraction of those that he could consume, then he engages in an act of saving, and he can now form some expectation as to how long it will take him to build a net, and what will be the output of fish, per hour, let's say, that he can attain with the help of a net. And based on his evaluation of the time lag—let's say it takes a week to build the net—and his expectation is that he will double or triple his output—he can now decide how much or how little he wants to save. If Robinson Crusoe has what we call a high degree of time preference, that is, he prefers present goods very highly over future goods, meaning saving presents a great sacrifice for him, then the process of saving will be relatively slow, and it will take quite a while before he has accumulated enough saved-up fish to be in a position to say that now I have saved enough fish to feed myself during the week that is necessary for me to build the net. And once the net comes into existence, then his standard of living goes up.

The same, of course, is true if he wants to move from stage two to stage three. Again, he would have to make an estimation of how long will it take him to build that fishing trawler, what will be the likely increase in productivity that he can achieve if he has the fishing trawler available, and then he determines how much or how little, in terms of saving, he is willing to do. Again, if his time preference is very high, preferring present satisfaction very much over future satisfaction, then the process of going from year to year will take a long time. If his time preference is very low, that is, he is willing to make larger sacrifices, then he can delay his future gratification more and save more, and the process of going from stage one to stage two, and from stage two to stage three, is shorter. Each step along the line, his standard of living increases. It should be clear from the outset that no one would engage in the construction of capital goods unless he expected that production with the help of a capital good will be more productive than production without a capital good. If I can produce ten fish per day by using my bare hands, and if by using a net I can also produce only ten fish per day, then obviously the net would never come into existence, because the entire time spent constructing the net would be nothing but sheer waste—that is, capital goods are always brought into existence with the expectation that production with capital goods is more productive than production without capital goods. Because of this, because of the productivity of capital goods, people are willing to pay a price for them. If the net did not yield a higher output per hour than using your bare hands, then obviously nobody would ever be willing to pay a price for the net. If the fishing trawler did not promise a larger output per hour than the net, then the price of the fishing trawler could not conceivably be higher than the price of the net, and so forth.

What holds men back, as far as investment and capital goods accumulation is concerned, is always time preference. We do not automatically choose the most productive method, but it is time preference, and, related to it, savings, that allows us or does not allow us to choose certain techniques or not to choose certain techniques. Let me, in order to illustrate this concept of time preference a little bit more, use some examples, some of which you'll find in Mises, some of which I developed. Let's assume we were like angels, who can live off love and air alone, that is, we have no need for consumption. We can imagine that an angel could in fact produce goods immediately and in the most productive fashion, even though the angel would not have any motive to produce at all; after all, he can live off love and air alone. But let's say he had some sort of fund to produce large amounts of goods. Because the angel could wait forever, the interest rate, the degree to which he prefers present goods to future goods, is zero; it doesn't make any difference to him whether he has a fish right now or a fish ten thousand years from now. For us, who are somewhat less than angelic, that does, of course, make a tremendous difference, whether we have fish ten thousand years from now or today or in one week. So, we are constrained by time preference; our interest rate is positive; it is higher than zero.

Take another example that helps illustrate this concept of time preference. Let's assume, for instance—this gets us already into some sort of cultural influence on this phenomenon of time preference and capital accumulation—let's assume, that we know that the world will end one week from now, and we are all perfectly certain that this is going to happen. What would then happen to the willingness to exchange present goods for future goods? And the answer is, of course, that this willingness would essentially disappear. The interest rate, in this case, would skyrocket. No interest payment would be high enough to induce anybody to sacrifice current consumption for a higher amount of future consumption because, after all, there is no future. There are, for instance, certain religious sects who believe that the world will soon go under, and very quickly the good guys will go to heaven and the bad guys will go someplace else. And these people, of course, stop saving. They will just have one more glorious week of consumption and then the whole story will be over.

As I said, all humans prefer present goods over future goods. But the degree to which people do this is different from individual to individual, and also from one specific group to another. Let me just give you a few examples, of which we know with pretty good certainty that their degree of time preference differs on average. Take little children, for instance. Little children have a very high degree of time preference. Another way to say it is that little children have tremendous difficulties delaying gratification. Promises of high rewards in the future do not necessarily induce children to make the current sacrifice of not consuming, of not satisfying current desires. There have been experiments done in this regard, such as: you give a dollar to a child and tell him that if you don't spend the dollar until tomorrow, I'll double the amount, you get another dollar. And if you then, tomorrow, have not spent $2, I will again, double it and give you $4, and so forth. You realize how high the interest rate here is, it's 100 percent per day. If you have a calculator, you can figure out what sort of annual interest rate that is. Nonetheless, you will find that many children are absolutely incapable of accepting a deal such as this. They have to rush out to the 7-Eleven and get their Big Gulp right now, even though they could have two Big Gulps or four Big Gulps in a very short distance in the future. Or, another way to illustrate this would be to say that we offer a child a perfectly secure certificate that promises to pay $100 one year from now, but the child has the choice of selling right now this perfectly safe and secure promise of $100 in the future. Then we will find that the children might be willing to sell this certificate for only 10 cents, because waiting is basically intolerable for them.

Let me give you a few other examples and you realize, of course, depending on what sort of mentality exists among the public, capital accumulation can take forever or it can go quite quickly. If Robinson Crusoe had a childlike mentality, he might never ever reach the second stage, or if he does reach it, it might take him about one hundred years to do so.

I will move on to some other examples of groups. Very old people are sometimes said to go through a "second childhood." This is not necessarily so, because very old people can choose to provide for future generations. But assuming that they do not care for future generations, or perhaps they do not have any offspring or any friends whom they want to hand over their own fortune to, and then, because their own remaining lifespan is very short, they have not much of a future left, so they go through the phase of a second childhood, by and large consuming and more or less entirely ceasing to accumulate any savings.

We can take the example of criminals, who are also, typically speaking—and I mean the normal run-of-the-mill-type criminal, not the white-collar-type criminal, the muggers, the murderers, the rapists and those friendly figures—characterized by high time preference. The way I explain this to my students is always using the following example. (Sometimes people hiss at it; most people like it.) Imagine a normal person who is in pursuit of a girl or vice versa, a girl in pursuit of a man. Then, what we do, of course, is take her out to dinner and bring her flowers and take her out to dinner again. We listen to the conversation; we are very impressed by all the deep thoughts that we hear. We have never heard anything interesting like that before in our lives. Of course, we entertain certain expectations, which are, of course, in the more or less distant future. This is how normal people operate. If you have a childlike mentality, but you have that in an adult body, then this sort of stuff is almost an impossible sacrifice; you cannot wait that long and then you become a rapist or something of that nature. Normally, in order to satisfy any desire, we have to work for a day, at least for a day. Then we get paid at the end of the day and then we can buy our beer. But, what if a day of waiting is too long? The only other alternative that you have is to look for some old lady and rob her of her purse and to satisfy your desires in this way.

I will give you another example that already touches upon a lecture that I will give later in the week. Democratic politicians also have a very high degree of time preference. They are in power for a very short period of time and what they do not loot right now, they will not be able to loot in five or six years. So, their intention is, of course, that I have to milk the public as much as possible now, because then, with a lot of tax income, I can make myself a lot of friends in the present, and who cares about the future?

The last example is one that has gotten me in deep trouble recently at my university. I have used that example for sixteen years or so and had never any problem with it whatsoever. This time, however, some fanatic wanted to bring me down; this whole process is still underway, so I warn you not to bring harassment suits against me again. I made the point that if you compare homosexuals to regular heterosexuals with families, you can say that homosexuals have a higher time preference because life ends with them. I always thought that that was so obvious, almost beyond dispute, and then pointed out in the next sentence, that this helps us understand, for instance, the attitude of a man like Keynes, whose economic philosophy was "in the long run, we are all dead." Now, this is true for some people, but it is not true for most people, who, of course, have their own children and so forth, future generations to come. As I said, these harmless remarks have led to three months of harassment at my university, and the whole thing is still not over yet.

So, so much about the concept of time preference. Now I want to say a few words about the development of time preference and of interest over time, in the course of history. As you can imagine, this is not difficult, but rather intuitively immediately clear. We would expect that the degree of time preference should gradually fall in the course of human history. Something like what you see in Figure 1:

FIGURE 1: HISTORIC LONG-TERM INTEREST RATES

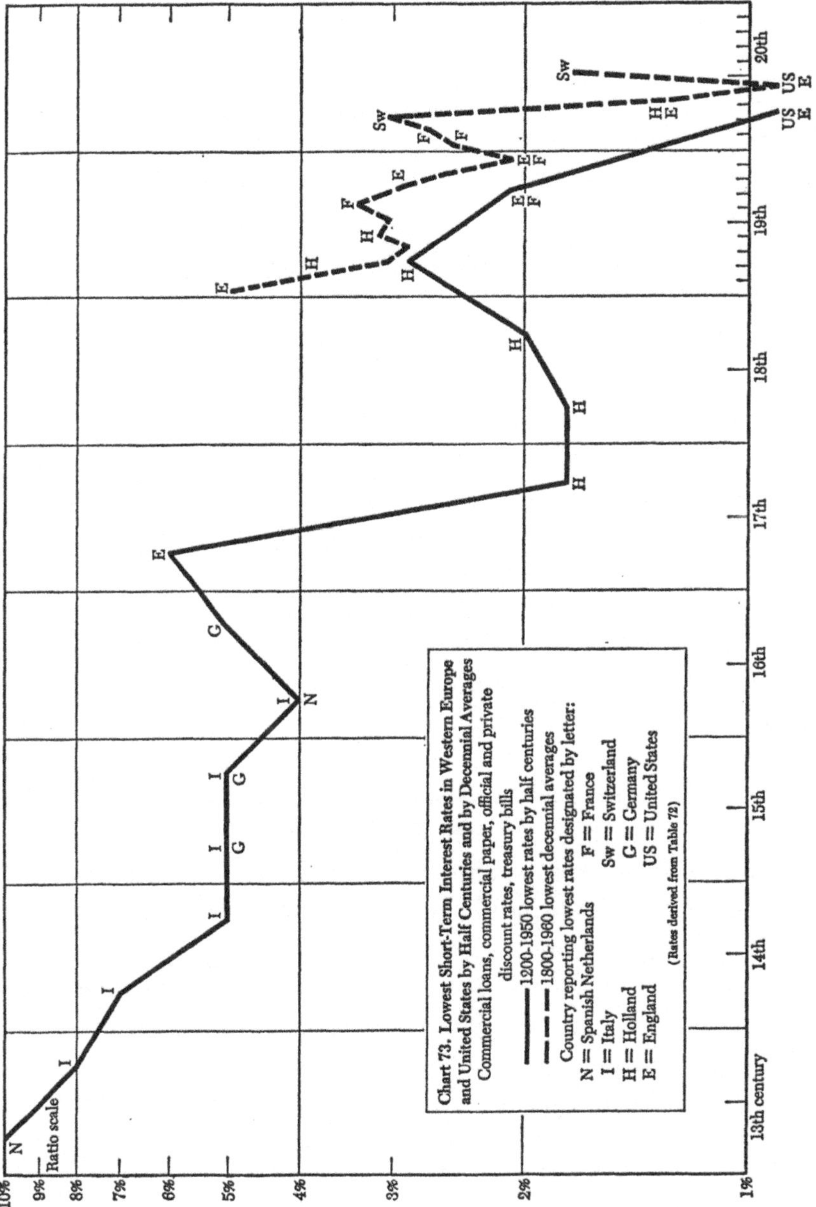

Sidney Homer, *A History of Interest Rates* (New Brunswick, NJ: Rutgers University Press, 1963), p. 507.

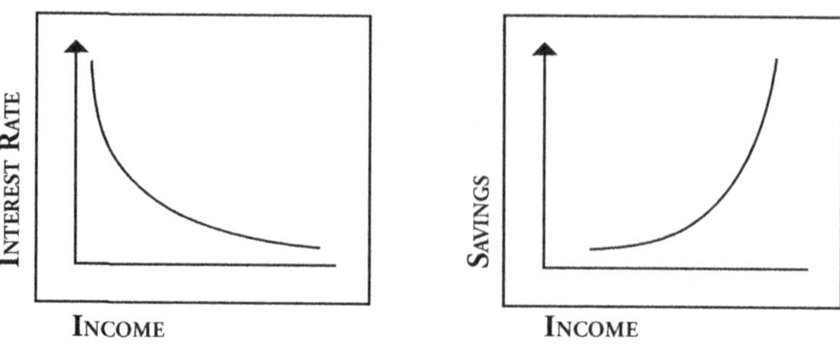

Figure 2: Income, Interest Rate, and Savings

Here in Figure 2 we have interest, or a degree of time preference, on one axis, and on the other axis we have real money income, that is, income that can be converted into immediate present satisfaction. Then we would expect that with very low real income, the sacrifice of exchanging a present good for a future good is very high, and people will save and invest only small amounts, but as real incomes rise, the interest rate will gradually tend to fall. That is, savings, the volume of saving and investing, will become greater; intuitively that is perfectly clear. For a rich man, it is easier to save and invest than it is for a poor man. If we look over the course of history, we would find that capital accumulation—savings and investment—does become successively easier. It is more difficult at the beginning of mankind as it requires a bigger sacrifice, and it becomes successively easier as we grow wealthier. This is something that we can indeed see in history. This has been studied—long-run interest rates for the safest possible investments and so forth—and we find, by and large, that interest rates fall.

Of course, there are exceptions to this rule. If you have wars and so forth, then you have an increase in interest rates, because the risk attached to loans becomes significantly higher. But, we also have certain periods when the degree of time preference does seem to rise. I will come back to that again in a later lecture. This seems to be something that has happened in the twentieth century. We should have expected that interest rates, real interest rates, in the twentieth century should be lower than in the nineteenth century, given that on the average, wealth in society is greater in the twentieth century than in the nineteenth. However, we do not find this to be true; that is, the real interest rates in the twentieth century rarely, if ever, reach the low point that they reached around 1900, which was about 2.25 percent. The conclusion would be that the entire time preference schedule must have risen in the twentieth century, which would amount to saying that the population in the twentieth century has become somewhat more childlike than the population in the nineteenth century. We are somewhat more frivolous and hedonistic in our lifestyle than our forefathers or our parents and our grandparents were, despite the fact that it was more difficult for them to engage in savings and capital accumulation than it is for us.

Now, a word about the accumulation of capital. Obviously, in every society, it is possible to add something to the existing stock of capital, to maintain the existing stock of capital or to deplete the existing stock of capital. Even to maintain the existing stock of capital, continued savings is necessary because all capital goods wear out over time. That is what we call capital consumption. Capital consumption, however, can take quite some time before it becomes visible, because some capital goods last for a long time. For instance, when the Communists took over Russia, they inherited a substantial stock of capital goods: machines, houses, etc.; and after that, they were still able to go on for a while, but if, due to the fact that no private property or factors of production existed anymore, practically no savings were forthcoming, you could expect that eventually this inherited stock of capital goods would become dilapidated and in some ten, twenty, or thirty years, you would experience some sort of catastrophe. And this is what happened: all the capital goods were suddenly worn out, and nothing was there to replace them. The same thing is true for the process of capital accumulation.

Let me first point out the following. Obviously, the amount of capital accumulation depends not just on the time preference that various individuals have; it depends also on the security of private property rights. Imagine Friday, a second person, coming onto the island. We can imagine Friday to be like Robinson Crusoe, and they engage in division of labor. Then, the standard of living would go up, capital accumulation would be even faster than with Robinson Crusoe being alone; standards of living go higher and so forth. But, we can also imagine that Friday is different, perhaps a mugger from Brooklyn, and he sees that Robinson Crusoe has already built the fishing net or has already saved all sorts of fish and he says, "This is very nice that you have done this already for me and I'll take the net, or I force you to pay a tax to me: half of the fish that you produce every day you will hand over to me." Now, in that situation, you can of course easily imagine that the process of capital accumulation will be drastically slowed down, or will even come to a complete standstill. If we look at societies that are currently rich, we cannot necessarily infer that those societies are societies in which property rights receive the best possible protection. What we can only infer is that these must be societies in which property rights must have been well protected in the past, and it might well be that we encounter societies that are quite poor right now but which do have very secure private property rights. Of those societies, we would expect that in the future they will show rapid rates of growth.

One might say, for instance, that to a large extent, the endowment in the United States of capital goods is due to circumstances that are long gone. That is, a lot of the capital goods have been accumulated under far more favorable circumstances than the circumstances that currently exist, and we might already be in a phase of gradual capital consumption without actually knowing it. It might take us decades before we actually find out that this is the case. As far as the United States itself is concerned, savings rates are atrociously low. To a large extent, the United States still benefits from the fact that there are savers from other countries who still consider the United States a good place to invest their funds, despite the fact that property rights are no longer nearly as safe as they were in the nineteenth century. Just keep in mind that almost 40 percent of the saved-up fish of Robinson Crusoe is nowadays handed over to the mugger from Brooklyn! In the nineteenth century, this might have been 2 percent or 3 percent of the output of Robinson Crusoe. In any case, capital needs to be preserved, and in order to preserve it, it is necessary that there exists an institutional legal framework that makes private property safe. If this framework is lacking, then one should not be surprised that very little takes place in terms of capital accumulation.

Just imagine a place where there is an impending Communist revolution, where you must be fearful that maybe in the next election, the Communists will come to power and the first thing that they will do is expropriate all owners of capital goods. Now, imagine what that does to your motivation to engage in saving and the accumulation of additional capital. Large parts of the world are like this. That is, we explain the poverty of many countries by the fact that property rights in those countries have, for many, many years, sometimes for centuries, not been secure enough for people to engage in saving and the accumulation of capital.

Now I want to come to some historical illustrations, and I want to use population growth and city growth as vague approximations of what happens to capital accumulation. Recall, accumulating more capital means societies become richer; societies becoming richer implies that larger population sizes can be sustained. And recall some of the numbers that I gave you in previous lectures. Fifty thousand people lived on Earth about 100,000 years ago. Five million people lived at the beginning of the Neolithic Revolution, 10,000 to 12,000 years ago. At the year 1 AD, the population is estimated to have been somewhere between 170 million and 400 million. There was a far more rapid growth of the population after the Neolithic Revolution, a doubling of the population every 1,300 years; until the Neolithic Revolution, a doubling of the population happened every 13,000 years or so. That is, again, a reflection of the fact that in agricultural societies, there is already a significantly increased amount of capital accumulation that allows this larger population to be sustained.

In Figure 3, you see estimates of world population, beginning at 400 BC and going almost to the present, until 2000. You see also the wide variety of estimates, with considerable disagreement, especially regarding the early periods of mankind. During the period beginning with the Neolithic Revolution, we see the development of various civilizations, indicating, obviously, sharp increases in the accumulation of capital goods. Table 1 gives you some sort of historical overview of these various civilizations, the beginning and the end, the name of the most dominant group, and finally the names of those groups that were responsible for the destruction of these civilizations. I already indicated in the previous lecture that in these early civilizations, Mesopotamia, Egypt, and China, we experienced for the first time major cities coming into existence, and we also have indications of specific new technologies being developed. Again, recall that it requires a certain amount

Figure 3
Total World Population
Units—measured in millions of people

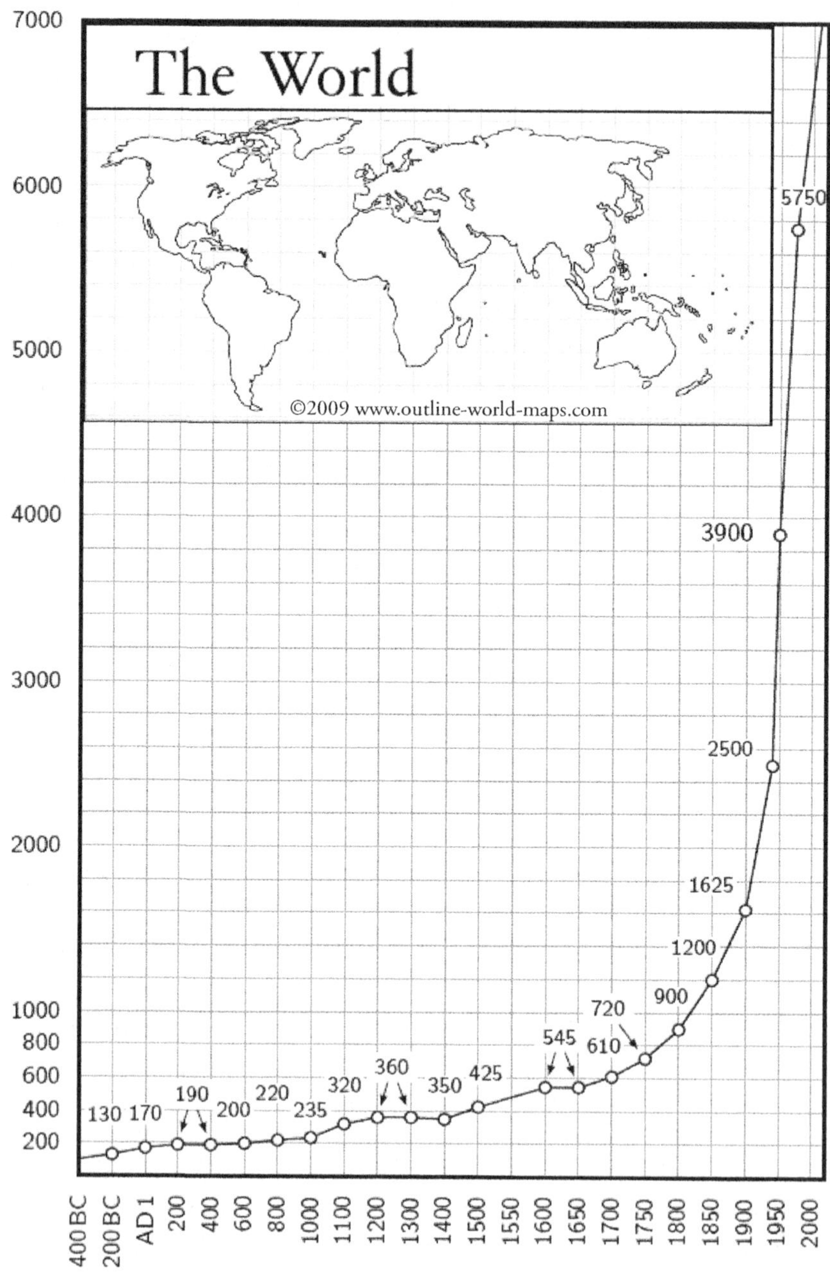

TABLE 1
CIVILIZATIONS, EMPIRES, AND INVADERS

NAME	DATES	EMPIRE	INVADERS
Mesopotamian	6000–300 B.C.	Persian	Greeks
Egyptian	5500–300 B.C.	Egyptian	Greeks
Indic	3500–1500 B.C.	Harappa	Aryans
Cretan	3000–1100 B.C.	Minoan	Dorians
Sinic	2000 B.C. – A.D. 400	Han	Huns
Hittite	1900–1000 B.C.	Hittite	Phrygians
Canaanite	2200–100 B.C.	Punic	Romans
Classical	1100 B.C. – A.D. 500	Roman	Germans
Mesoamerican	1000 B.C. – A.D. 1550	Aztec	Europeans
Andean	1500 B.C. – A.D. 1600	Inca	Europeans
Hindu	1500 B.C. – A.D. 1900	Mogul	Europeans
Islamic	600–1940	Ottoman	Europeans
Chinese	400–1930	Manchu	Europeans
Japanese	100 B.C.–A.D. 1950 (?)	Tokugawa	Europeans
Orthodox	600–	Soviet	?
Western	500–	?	?

Reproduced from Carroll Quigley, *The Evolution of Civilizations: An Introduction to Historical Analysis* (1961; Indianapolis, IN: LibertyPress, 1979), p. 84.

of wealth and capital accumulation to allow people to develop new inventions and try out new things.

Just to give you some examples of the major technological capital goods developments that took place during the Babylonian civilization, that is in the period of 4500 BC to 2500 BC. Here we find *plows* used for the first time; we find *wheeled carts* for the first time; we find *draft animals* being used in agriculture; we find *bricks* being used for the first time, and magnificent *buildings* erected. We find what is quite unique and has not been repeated independently anywhere else in history, the invention of *the arch*, which allows, of course, construction of structures that otherwise would collapse under their own weight. And we know the arch concept was imported to other areas. We find the *potter's wheel.* We find *copper smelting.* We find the development of *bronze*, which is a combination of tin and copper in certain combinations. We find the development of *writing*, which indicates that there must have been a class of intellectuals in existence, who can only be supported if there exists a certain amount of wealth in society. And a certain amount of wealth, of course, requires a certain amount of capital accumulation. We find quite far developed *mathematical techniques* in Babylonia, and we find traces of *metallic money* being used. And obviously in the cities, which reached sizes of 80,000 people or so, we had quite an extent of *specialized professions* coming forth.

But, as I said, there exist in history also periods that we can describe as economic disintegration; that is, some of these empires fall apart. There are invaders that destroy them, and the division of labor shrinks. Techniques that were once known become forgotten, and we would expect them, during those periods also, to experience a decline in population. If you look at the estimates of world population there, you find, for instance, that only from 1000 AD on do we again see something like a trend toward an increase in the population, whereas with the fall of Rome, shortly after 200 AD or so, we see by and large a stagnation in the overall population. For almost one thousand years, there is virtually no population growth that takes place. And even in the period after 1000 AD, there are some centuries that see a more or less significant decline. Look, for instance, at the thirteenth century: from 1200 to 1300 AD, there appears to be no increase in world population, indicating capital consumption taking place or at least no capital accumulation taking place; even more clearly, look at the fifteenth century, that is the 1400s: there is a clear decline during this century in terms of population, as compared to the previous century, and it takes almost two hundred years or so before the population size is reached again that had already been reached in the fourteenth century. And once again, look at the seventeenth century, which is the century of the Thirty Years' War. Compare the numbers from 1600 to 1650, and you find that again there is a significant decline in population, which indicates, in this case, major wars and major destruction. And only from 1650 on do we see an uninterrupted rise in the population numbers. From 1650 to 1850, the doubling of the population required about two hundred years. Then, from 1850 to 1950, the doubling of the population is about every hundred years and after 1950, the doubling requires less than fifty years.

Another interesting topic in all this is to look at the growth of cities. Again, city growth being a rough indicator of what happens to capital accumulation. Before the year 1600, the ten or eleven largest cities were outside of Europe, they were: Beijing, which had more than 700,000; Istanbul, which had about 700,000; Agra in India, 500,000; Cairo, 400,000; Osaka, 400,000; Canton, 350,000; Edo, which is, I think, Tokyo, 350,000; Kyoto, also 350,000; Hangchow, 350,000, Lahore, 350,000, and Nanking, somewhat above 300,000. That corresponds, roughly, with what we know about the world. Until 1500 or so, there is absolutely no doubt that China was far more developed as a civilization than Western Europe. I will explain in later lectures what might be the causes of why this changed. Interestingly, the rapid growth of European cities, which were at this time small compared to Asian cities, sprang up in large numbers from about 1500 on, this rapid growth was unsurpassed by Asian cities.

Table 2 lists the thirty largest cities in Europe in the period from 1050 to 1800 AD. First, take a look at the total numbers at the very bottom and you see, of course, that the total numbers always go up, but they go up in a particularly drastic way only from about 1650 AD on, and before then the growth was comparatively moderate. But, if we take a look at specific cities, we can see in which way the centers of economic development changed: which places lost in significance, where obviously political events must have taken place that were unfavorable to capital accumulation, and how other places show a rapid increase in their ranks among the top thirty places. Let me just pick out a few cities here. Córdoba was the biggest city in 1050 AD. (The populations of Córdoba and Palermo are 450,000 and 350,000, respectively, and are somewhat in dispute as is noted in the table footnote, so I included the more realistic numbers of 150,000 and 120,000, respectively, for these two cities. Otherwise, that seems to be somewhat disproportionate.)

But, in any case, Córdoba, the biggest city in 1050 AD, has completely dropped out of the top thirty by 1500 AD. That's a general tendency that we can say, that Spanish cities, or even more general, Southern European cities, lost increasingly in significance, and the center of economic development and capital accumulation shifted to the north. Take some other spectacular cities here—Palermo, for instance, which you realize is the second-biggest city around 1000 AD, has no

Table 2
The Thirty Largest Cities in Europe by Population 1050–1800 (in Thousands)

c. 1050		c. 1200		c. 1330		c. 1500		c. 1650		c. 1800	
Cordova*	450/150	Palermo	150	Granada	150	Paris	225	Paris	400	London	948
Palermo*	350/120	Paris	110	Paris	150	Naples	125	London	350	Paris	550
Seville	90	Seville	80	Venice	110	Milan	100	Naples	300	Naples	430
Salerno	50	Venice	70	Genoa	100	Venice	100	Lisbon	150	Vienna	247
Venice	45	Florence	60	Milan	100	Granada	70	Venice	140	Amsterdam	217
Regensberg	40	Granada	60	Florence	95	Prague	70	Milan	120	Dublin	200
Toledo	37	Cordova	60	Seville	90	Lisbon	65	Amsterdam	120	Lisbon	195
Rome	35	Cologne	50	Cordova	60	Tours	60	Rome	110	Berlin	172
Barbastro	35	León	40	Naples	60	Genoa	58	Madrid	100	Madrid	168
Cartagena	33	Ypres	40	Cologne	54	Ghent	55	Palermo	100	Rome	153
Naples	30	Rome	35	Palermo	51	Florence	55	Seville	80	Palermo	140
Mainz	30	Bologna	35	Siena	50	Palermo	55	Florence	74	Venice	138
Mérida	30	Toledo	35	Barcelona	48	Rome	55	Vienna	70	Milan	135
Almeria	27	Verona	33	Valencia	44	Bordeaux	50	Granada	70	Hamburg	130
Granada	26	Narbonne	31	Toledo	42	Lyon	50	Marseille	70	Lyon	109
Speyer	25	Salerno	30	Bruges	40	Orleans	50	Copenhagen	65	Copenhagen	101
Palma	25	Pavia	30	Málaga	40	London	50	Genoa	64	Marseille	101
Laon	25	Messina	30	Aquila	40	Bologna	50	Bologna	63	Barcelona	100
London	25	Naples	30	Bologna	40	Verona	50	Antwerp	60	Seville	96
Elvira	22	Genoa	30	Cremona	40	Brescia	49	Brussels	60	Bordeaux	96
Cologne	21	Angers	30	Pisa	38	Cologne	45	Lyon	60	Genoa	90
Trier	20	Palma	30	Ferrara	36	Seville	45	Rouen	60	Manchester	84
Caen	20	Speyer	30	London	35	Marseille	45	Danzig	60	Edinburgh	83
Lyon	20	Worms	28	Montpellier	35	Málaga	42	Leiden	55	Turin	82
Paris	20	Ferrara	27	Rouen	35	Valencia	42	Valencia	50	Florence	81
Tours	20	Orleans	27	St.-Omer	35	Ferrara	42	Prague	50	Valencia	80
Verona	20	Metz	27	Lisbon	35	Rouen	40	Hamburg	40	Rouen	80
Worms	20	Valencia	26	Angers	33	Cremona	40	Cologne	40	Nantes	77
Lisbon	15	Cremona	25	Marseille	31	Nuremburg	38	Nuremburg	40	Stockholm	76
Florence	15	London	25	Toulouse	30	Bruges	35	Ghent	40	Prague	76

Source: The Bairoch database. See Paul Bairoch, Jean Bateau, and Pierre Chèvre, *La population des villes Européenes: Banque de données et analyse sommaire des résultats, 800–1850* / (*The Population of European Cities: Data Bank and Short Summary of Results*) (1988). *Russell's estimates of the populations of Cordova and Palermo in 1050 are only one-third as large. *Reproduced from* J. Bradford DeLong and Andrei Shleifer, "Princes and Merchants: European City Growth before the Industrial Revolution," *Journal of Law and Economics* 36, no. 2 [October 1993]: 678.)

more inhabitants in 1800 AD than it had in the year 1000. Obviously, Palermo was not exactly the center of economic development during this time, but rather was a dying city. The same is also true for Seville. Again, Seville ranks number three in 1000 AD and hundreds of years later has a population that is not in any significant way larger. Then look at the spectacular rise of Florence until 1330 AD. So, Florence is the lowest one in the first column, with 15,000 in the year 1000, and then moves rapidly up the rank order until about 1330 AD, where the population has increased from 15,000 to 95,000, and then a decline of Florence takes place. Look at the spectacular growth of London, which, in the last column, of course, is by far the biggest European city. In the previous column, it is the second biggest. In the year 1500 column, it has just 50,000 inhabitants and in 1330 AD, only 35,000 inhabitants. So, in this period from 1330 to 1800 AD, we see a spectacular rise of London, again, indicating, obviously, a very favorable climate for capital accumulation that existed there.

And interesting are also some cases of decline. For instance, there is a very quick rise and a very quick fall of Bruges (or Brügge), in what would be Belgium today. And then, the city of Bruges, after it falls, obviously the economic environment becomes very unfriendly. We see then, as a substitute, a very quick rise in the city size of Ghent, a neighboring city, which indicates to what extent neighboring cities competed against each other for capital accumulation and for merchants settling in those cities. And again, Ghent falls very quickly, to be overtaken by another city very close by, namely Antwerp. And then, Antwerp also falls very quickly and then we see the spectacular rise of Amsterdam, again, a city very close to Antwerp, again illustrating in this case the mobility of capital, people leaving one place because it offers less favorable conditions for capital accumulation and moving to other places not far away and exhibiting there a spectacular growth. A similar spectacular growth you find, for instance, in the city of Hamburg.

LECTURE 5

The Wealth of Nations: Ideology, Religion, Biology, and Environment

---

BESIDES PURELY ECONOMIC FACTORS, SUCH as the division of labor, money and capital accumulation, ideological factors also play a very important role in economic development and in the formation of societies. Ideological factors, in a way, even influenced such fundamental things as the attitude toward the division of labor in a given society, and in particular also the attitude toward capital accumulation, the desire to become wealthier or to be satisfied with low standards of living. I want to spend this lecture discussing certain ideological factors, mostly religious factors, influencing economic development.

I will start by reminding you that capital accumulation and—based on capital accumulation—the desire to make inventions, technological improvements and so forth, can be encouraged or can be discouraged by certain prevalent ideologies existing in society. Before I start talking about major religions, let me just give you some examples that make this intuitively clear. Imagine, for instance, if people believed in a deity that leaves the world with the instruction that things should be left the way they are. If such a religion were a powerful religion among people, you can easily imagine that such a society would not have much of a potential to develop and become prosperous. We would likely guess that societies such as this would tend to die out, or will be taken over by other societies. Or, imagine a society that has a very deep and profound ancestor worship. Of such a society, we would expect that it will display, to a large extent, very ritualistic behavior, and that it also will be reluctant to introduce any innovations.

The same is also true for slave societies. Of course in many parts of the world, for large parts of human history, we did have slave societies. The most prominent examples would be classical civilization, Greek and Roman civilizations, and also the more recent example of the United States. In slave societies, it is frequently the case that the slaves do the work and the masters laze around, don't do much, are not involved in the day-to-day activities, and because they are not involved in the day-to-day activities, they also contribute little to improvements in the technology that can be employed in these day-to-day activities. Let me give you a brief quote from Carroll Quigley to this effect. He writes,

> Suppose that the primitive tribe believes that its social organization was established by a deity who went away leaving strict instruction that nothing be changed. Such a society would invent very little. Egyptian civilization was something like that. Or any society that had ancestor worship would probably have weak incentives to invent. Or a society whose productive system was based on slavery, would probably be uninventive. Slave societies, such as classical civilization or the Southern states of the United States in the period before 1860, have been notoriously uninventive. No major inventions in the field of production came from either of these civilizations.[1]

This is not to say that these civilizations did not develop other achievements. Obviously, the Greek civilization allowed a class of philosophers to emerge, and they passed on another form of inheritance to us, namely

---

[1]Carroll Quigley, *The Evolution of Civilizations*, 2d ed. (Indianapolis, IN: Liberty Fund, 1979), p. 134.

that of rigorous logic or thinking, which has had a tremendous impact on human development. But when it comes to improving existing tools that one uses in production, they were indeed very unproductive.

Let me give a few other examples that will show how certain ideologies might prevent wealth from being accumulated in societies. There exist religions, for instance, that prescribe that whenever the master of a household dies, that he should be buried with all of his possessions. That seems to be, from the outset, a very stupid attitude, at least as far as ever making any progress is concerned; every generation would destroy whatever they have accumulated during that generation.

Or imagine societies that are ridden by feelings of envy. There exist numerous examples of this which you can find, for instance, in the famous book *Envy* by the German sociologist Helmut Schoeck. And you also find many examples, some of them taken from the Schoeck book, in Rothbard's little book on *Egalitarianism as a Revolt against Nature*. Again, I just want to quote one example of a society such as this, from Herbert Spencer. Spencer writes,

> [There exist reports about the chiefs among the Abipones, of the Dakotas:] The cacique has nothing either in his arms or his clothes to distinguish him from a common man, except the peculiar oldness and shabbiness of them. For, if he appears in the streets with new and handsome apparel, the first person he meets will boldly cry, "Give me that dress" and unless he immediately parts with it, he becomes the scoff and scorn of all and hears himself called covetous.[2]

Obviously, a society like this is not likely to accumulate much in terms of wealth. Or, there exist societies where as soon as the big chief has accumulated a certain amount of foodstuffs or other goods, he is obliged to throw a big party for the entire tribe and at this big party, all of the resources that have been accumulated will be wasted away. That is, a continuous process of capital accumulation simply does not take place in societies such as this. Now, it can be safely assumed that these

---

[2]Herbert Spencer, *Principles of Sociology*, 2nd ed. (New York: D. Appleton Co., 1916), p. 557.

types of examples that I give, are obviously not examples of societies that we would expect to stand the test of time, to last very long, but instead, being displaced by other societies that have different attitudes, and either defeat them in the form of warfare or simply displace them. That is, just make them leave or push them out of the territories that they inhabit to more unhabitable territories, and then they ultimately die out.

What I now want to do is undertake a survey of the major religions and their attitudes toward work and invention and capital accumulation. I'm not interested in the pure theological part of these religions, just in those parts of the religions that have repercussions for the day-to-day conduct that people are expected to engage in.

I will begin with one of the religions that is comparatively bad, when it comes to capital accumulation, inventiveness and so forth, and that is Hinduism. Hinduism is characterized, as far as its economic doctrines are concerned, first by explicit taboos against using certain resources. As you all know, for instance, cows cannot be used, and there exist other taboos that simply make it impossible for resources that could have been put to some useful employment to be used this way. In addition, Hinduism is a religion that is characterized by strict association taboos. That is to say, certain groups of people are not allowed to associate with certain other types of people, and you immediately recognize that this is, of course, quite an obstacle when it comes to the development of the division of labor. What you would expect of such a society, a society of castes that are prevented from having any systematic contact with each other, is that there will be some sort of petrification of production modes. Each caste sticks to its own techniques and tasks that are assigned to it, and there is no interchange of ideas; there is no social mobility of any kind and this, obviously, has negative repercussions as far as the economic growth potential is concerned. In addition, Hinduism requires strict obedience to the rules of the caste and has in place severe obstacles in the way of any economic progress. There is the promise of reincarnation into higher classes, which leads the lower classes to not rebel against the existing caste system, because rebelling against the existing caste system will prevent you from being reincarnated into a higher caste in a future life.

There is also—this has to do with taboos with respect to certain objects—the problem that there is no clear-cut distinction in the rank of creatures on Earth. Recall, for instance, in Christianity, in Genesis, we learn that man is the highest of all creatures and that he is given dominion over the rest of the world. On the other hand, if you have a religion that does not necessarily see mankind as the highest development having dominion over the animals, but that there are gradual differences between the animal kingdom and the human kingdom, then again, this is something that hampers the economic growth potential. It leads also to widespread vegetarianism, and widespread vegetarianism, despite the fact that there are some people who propagate it even in our societies, is certainly not a lifestyle that energizes you and makes you an entrepreneurial person, if you only just eat grain.

Hinduism also permits human sacrifice, which further indicates that the status of humans is not above everybody else. And it encourages orgies, that is, activities that display a high degree of time preference, having fun right now, just overdoing it completely, not disciplining yourself during these orgiastic experiences. On the other hand, they also emphasize pomp, that is the display of riches, and do not do what we will see later on, especially in puritanical religions, that is, you don't live a pompous life; you are humble and invest, but don't display for everyone how well off you are. And, in general, it is a religion that encourages submission—submission of certain groups vis-à-vis other groups. So, if we rank various religions, we can say from the outset that Hinduism, as long as people really adhere to it, is not exactly a religion that has great economic promises in store. And in a way, looking at India, we can see that that is borne out by the facts. In addition, India has also adopted another system, namely mass democracy, which contributes to their lack of economic promise, but this is a modern development. Traditional India, of course, was not democratic, by any means.

Let us then take another Eastern religion, Buddhism. And to a lesser extent, what applies to Buddhism also applies to Daoism. Buddhism started in a way as a reform movement of Hinduism, but essentially disappeared from India itself, and instead gained influence in Southeast Asia, outside of the Indian subcontinent. The Buddhist view of life is that ultimate wisdom consists in detachment from life, from the earthly, worldly life. It views life as painful, and it considers an ascetic lifestyle as a means to eliminate or to reduce the pain that comes from regular life. So, it advocates a life of ascetic meditation. Again, it should be perfectly clear that for people to withdraw from the world is not encouraging the type of attitude that we consider to be normal. The goal of the Buddhist religion is Nirvana, and Nirvana is a state of affairs that brings about the elimination of all desires. Now of course, if you try to eliminate all your human desires, then there will be little need to engage in productive activities, which are those activities that we consider to be necessary in order to reduce our pains. The essence and purpose of life for the Buddhist and also for the Daoist, to a certain extent, is not individual fulfillment and especially not individual fulfillment in this life. The life that anyone is living right now is just one of thousands of lives. So, there is very little emphasis on personal happiness, or on individual achievement. Daoism teaches the serene acceptance and humility and gentleness and passivity and understanding acceptance of whatever happens to occur, rather than individual accomplishment and individual advancement. Again, the empirical evidence bears that clearly out, that devoted Buddhist societies are not exactly highly developed societies.

Let me come to the next major religion, Islam. Islam also does not in any way encourage individual autonomy. As a matter of fact, the translation of the word "Islam" is "submission." And what we frequently hear from proponents of Islam, is that they point out this golden age of Islam during the time that they occupied Spain, during which they rescued some of the achievements that were generated by the classical Greek culture and they then transmitted them to Christianity. But this so-called golden age is more of an exception, a fluke in Islam, than typical of the Islamic religion. The main proponents during this era, the main Islamic intellectuals of this era, were by and large intellectuals that had broken with orthodox Islam and were regarded with the utmost suspicion by the Islamic community at their time. So, it was only by breaking away from orthodox Islamic beliefs that these sorts of achievements became possible. The Islamic religion is very familistic, that is family-oriented, and rigidly hierarchically structured (not unlike the Chinese societies, to which I will come in a little bit.) Again, the hierarchical structure can be seen in particular in the relationships between males and females; females are clearly members of society with significantly fewer rights than males have.

In Islam, science and reason are not recognized as in Christianity, as a gift from God. They are not regarded as valuable in and of themselves, as they are, for instance, in Thomism, that is, in certain branches of Christianity. Rather, Islam views life on Earth as something that has no inherent or internal purpose, but it is mostly a preparation for the eternal life that comes afterward. In this regard, Islam is not all that different from very early Christianity, which also had a similar belief that life on Earth was of relatively minor importance and the main goal of it was just for the preparation for life after death. This is, of course, not characteristic of later Christianity, but in the early stages of Christianity, this sort of attitude did prevail. In the view of Islam, God, after the creation of the world, does not really retreat. The Christian view is that God creates a world and then he lets things happen, then mankind is on their own. Now, they have to prove themselves. From the point of view of Islam, God remains continuously involved in worldly affairs. But if God remains continuously involved in earthly affairs, this then makes the search for universal and eternal laws some sort of sinful behavior, almost blasphemous. If you think that God retreats and then lets the world run the way he has organized it, then, of course, it makes sense to try to figure out what the laws of the world are, but if God remains involved in earthly affairs, then, in a way, it doesn't make any sense to even look out for universal regularities. As a matter of fact, to stipulate that there are universal regularities, is some sort of insult against the belief that God remains continuously involved in earthly affairs. So, this is considered to be somewhat a vain activity and to almost denying God's almightiness.

What should be perfectly clear from the outset is that if, and to the extent that, these beliefs are the beliefs of the overwhelming majority of the people, then you should expect little in terms of scientific and scholarly achievement coming from such societies. The achievements coming from these societies, as I mentioned, are mostly produced by individuals who have somehow broken with the basic tenets of the religion. On this subject let me quote a German anthropologist who writes on this feature of Islam. His name is von Grünebaum, and he says that Islam was never able to accept that scientific research is a means of glorifying God.

> Those accomplishments of Islamic mathematical and medical sciences which continue to compel our admiration were developed in areas and in periods where the elites were willing to go beyond and possibly against the basic strains of orthodox thought and feeling. For the sciences never shed the suspicion of bordering on the impious....This is why the pursuit of the natural sciences, as that of philosophy, tended to become located in relatively small and esoteric circles and why but few of their representatives would escape an occasional uneasiness...which not infrequently did result in some kind of apology for their own work.[3]

Now, after Islam, also not exactly favorable to economic development and again, something that is borne out by the facts, we come now to Confucianism. And Confucianism, we have to admit from the outset, is far more suitable for economic growth; it has a far more positive attitude toward science and investigation and is, in a way, a very interesting case. Keep in mind that until 1500 or so, China was clearly the most developed region on the globe. Confucianism is entirely realistic in its outlook and entirely this-worldly. It has no anthropomorphic concept of a god. It does speak of heavens, but the heavens are some sort of impersonal thing. It has nothing to do with what we imagine God to be, which has, of course, some sort of manly image. They actually do not have a concept of a deity. They also have no promise of an afterlife. That can be an advantage, or it can be a disadvantage: that depends in a way on how other religions depict the afterlife. But, in any case, no promise of an afterlife is given. The entirely realistic and rationalistic attitude of Confucianism is also reflected in the fact that there exist no miracles for them, in contrast to Christianity, where we admit the existence of miraculous events. Miraculous events do not exist for Confucians. That is, everything can be rationally explained. And accordingly, there also

[3]G. E. von Grünebaum, *Islam: Essays in the Nature and Growth of a Cultural Tradition* (1955; Whitefish, MT: Kessinger Publishing, 2010).

exists no such thing as a saint. Confucius himself is neither a god, nor is he a prophet. Confucius is just a leader, a teacher. Because of this, some people have even doubted whether it is appropriate to refer to Confucianism as a religion. That is, without a god, without a prophet, can we legitimately refer to it as a religion? Let me, at this moment, give you a quote from Stanislav Andreski on Confucianism. Stanislav Andreski is a Polish sociologist who taught most of his life in England, and he is one of those very few sociologists who is not a leftist. There are a few others like Robert Nisbet and Helmut Schoeck. As I said, Stanislav Andreski is very interesting.[4] He writes on Confucianism,

> If we want to rank the religions in accordance with their compatibility with the findings of science, we must place Confucianism far ahead in first place. Indeed, its rationalistic and this-worldly outlook has led some scholars to deny that it is a religion. None the less, it certainly is a religion in the etymological sense (which is derived from the Latin word "to bind") because it undoubtedly did constitute a bond which united many millions during two millennia. However, if we include an anthropomorphic concept of deity and a promise of life after death as essential characteristics of a religion, then we have to conclude that Confucianism was not a religion because to the Confucians, the supreme entity is the Heavens—an invisible and impersonal force rather than a personalized god modeled on the image of a terrestrial despot as in the religions born in the Near East.
>
> When asked about what happens after death, Confucius replied, "When you don't know enough about the living, how can you know about the dead?" He never claimed, nor was attributed posthumously by

[4]I recommended sociologist Stanislav Andreski. In addition to his general books, I want to mention one in particular, one that is also a hilarious book. It is called *Social Sciences as Sorcery*. It makes fun of the sociology profession in general. If you have not read that book, I highly recommend it. It is something that you should read late at night before you go to bed and you will laugh yourself to sleep. It is a wonderful book and it's all you need to know about sociology.

> his followers, any powers which could be called supernatural or magical. The Confucians expect no miracles, have no saints and revere their founder not as a deity but as a great teacher. [5]

So, we can say that Confucianism is certainly a world outlook that is clearly compatible with capitalism. It has a very strong emphasis on filial piety, on family solidarity, and that might have some sort of negative effect when it comes to individual inventiveness with respect to breaking out of existing traditions, but in principle, of course, filial piety and familialism is nothing that is incompatible with capitalism. Again, let me, as regards to this lack of innovative spirit that you can find among the Confucians, give you a quote from Charles Murray, out of his book *Human Accomplishment: The Pursuit of Excellence*, which I think captures this idea quite well. He says,

> At the core of the Confucian ethic was the quality called *ren*, the supreme virtue in man—a quality that combines elements of goodness, benevolence and love. This ethic was most essential for those with the most power. "He who is magnanimous wins the multitude," Confucius taught. "He who is diligent attains his objective, and he who is kind can get service from the people." Indeed, to be a gentleman—another key concept in Confucian thought—required one above all to embody ren. And lest one think that a gentleman could get by with mouthing the proper platitudes, Confucius added, "The gentleman first practices what he preaches and then preaches what he practices."[6]

Now, Chinese and Japanese children also, to a certain extent, are then, because of this strong family orientation, supposed to make their life decisions always mindful of first, the wishes and the welfare of their parents, then of their extended family, and finally of their community.

---

[5]Stanislav Andreski, *Max Weber's Insights and Errors* (1984; London: Routledge, 2006), chap. 5, sec. 3.

[6]Charles Murray, *Human Accomplishment: The Pursuit of Excellence in the Arts and Sciences, 800 B.C. to 1950* (New York: HarperCollins, 2003), pp. 41–42.

There is a lack of encouragement for achieving one's own fulfillment no matter what, something that you do find to a far larger extent, of course, in the Western tradition. In addition, there is great emphasis on learning among the Chinese; China is a meritocratic system, where people from all walks of life, from all ranks, can, through some sort of examination system, reach the highest levels of society. That is, it is a society that, in a way, selects for high IQs, and thereby also tends to bind the population to the earthly powers. It is because everyone can rise and there is a meritocratic system that makes it appear fair who rises and who doesn't rise, even the lower strata of society are somehow consoled to live with this system.

What must be said as one of the explanations for why China nonetheless was not able to compete ultimately with the West, was the connection that existed between Confucianism and the state bureaucracies from very early on. That is, you did have, as you will see that we don't have in the West, an immediate or a more or less direct identity between the earthly rulers (the Chinese emperor) and the top hierarchies of the Confucian doctrine, of the Confucian theology, for lack of a better word. So, Confucianism had tied its forces very early on to the state, and because of that, the inherent reluctance to invent and to innovate was further strengthened.

Again, I point this out. This combination of Confucianism with the state led to a certain amount of uncritical thinking, that is, what we know in the West and what we have learned in the West in particular, from the Greeks, to present an argument and then a counterargument and then another counterargument and try to hammer out what is right and what is wrong, try to refute each other in an endless game of back and forth, this is something that you rarely find among the Chinese. I must say, based on my personal experience (because we have lots of Oriental students in Nevada), I can even detect this among my students whenever it comes to writing critical essays. They are always extremely good when they do mathematical equations and multiple choice, they remember everything, they always rank on top of the class. But when it comes to writing pieces like we learned it in school, you have the thesis and then you have to present the counterarguments and then you have to filter out what arguments are stronger and which ones are weaker and possibly synthesize this sort of stuff in some way, they do show a significant weakness in this department. Another indicator for this—again, this is a little bit speculative—is while you do find a massive overrepresentation of Orientals in fields like mathematics, physics, engineering and so forth, they are significantly underrepresented in law schools. And in law schools is precisely where this sort of Greek-style arguing is, that we all in the West have learned from elementary school on. But, where this Greek style of arguing is in particularly high demand they are underrepresented, as compared with other fields where they are clearly overrepresented. Again, a brief quote from Charles Murray on this observation. He says about East Asia,

> In the sciences, the disapproval of open dispute took a toll on the ability of East Asian science to build an edifice of cumulative knowledge....[T]he history of Chinese science is episodic, with the occasional brilliant scholarly discovery but no follow up. Progress in science in the West has been fostered by enthusiastic, nonstop, competitive argument in which the goal is to come out on top. East Asia did not have the cultural wherewithal to support enthusiastic, nonstop, competitive arguments. Even in today's Japan, a century and a half after the nation began Westernizing, it is commonly observed that Japan's technological feats far outweigh its slender body of original discoveries. One ready explanation for this discrepancy is the difference between progress that can be made consensually and hierarchically versus progress that requires individuals who insist that they alone are right.[7]

And of course you can tell that in the West there are plenty of people who think that they are right, that nobody else is right.

Now, from Confucianism, we will go to Judaism. From the outset, we will have to say that Judaism was always a very small and dispersed group of people, and as such they had in a way very little influence on the modern world. In addition, because they are a nonproselytizing

---

[7]Ibid., pp. 398–99.

religion, that is, they do not try to go on missions and convince other people to convert to their religion, they always remained a small group, dispersed over many places, with relatively limited influence. There are some people, such as German socialist Werner Sombart, one of the opponents of Ludwig von Mises, one of the so-called Katheder socialists, who advanced the thesis that the Jews were the inventors of modern capitalism, but this thesis is clearly false, for the following reason. Yes, it is true, for instance, that Holland, Venice, and a city like Frankfurt flourished after the influx of Jews into these places, and it is also true that after the expulsion of the Jews from Spain, Spain declined, but this does not necessarily show any causal relationship. There are also contrary examples. For instance, in Britain, industrial capitalism arose precisely during the period after the Jews were expelled from England and before they were readmitted to England, which shows that their presence was by no means necessary in order to develop capitalist institutions.

And there are other indicators that go in a different direction. For instance, wherever you had large numbers of Jews in the population, that is, wherever Jews were not a teeny-tiny minority surrounded by a different culture, as was the case, for instance, in Eastern Europe, there, the economic development was always negative. That is, there the Jewish presence went hand-in-hand with abject poverty. The Jews were more numerous in the backward countries like Poland and Russia, than they were in the advanced countries, Germany, France, and England.

When they begin to make major contributions to science, of course, nobody doubts this. This takes place only when they are small minorities in contact with dominant cultures surrounding them. For instance, in the Middle East, in Spain, during the so-called golden age of Arab rule and in particular, after the emancipation of the Jews by the Christians from the late eighteenth century on. I should emphasize that the emancipation of the Jews is a Christian achievement. The Jews were emancipated from their own rule and not by themselves, but by external forces, by Christians, no longer being willing, so to speak, to oppress them and treat them in the way that they were treated by their own. So, before the year 1800, you see comparatively little in terms of achievements coming from Jews, and the achievements that you do see are typically by people who had broken with their religion.

Traditional Orthodox Judaism requires, again, a rigid subordination to your family and to your community, not quite unlike what you find in Islamic societies. In the so-called ghettos there existed self-administration of the Jews, and this self-administration was frequently typically given to them by the outside ruler in exchange for paying the outside ruler a part of the fines that the rabbis imposed internally on their own community. The Jews living in ghettos had something to do with the fact that some of their taboos involved that they had to live very close to the synagogue and could not work during certain periods of the day, so they had to be in close proximity to certain places. They could not live widely dispersed from each other, at least if you were an Orthodox Jew.

In Spain, for instance, that was precisely the arrangement. You get self-administration in your ghetto; you can impose any type of fine, any type of punishment that Rabbinical Law allows to be imposed on other Jews, but a certain percentage of the money collected you have to give to the Spanish king. So, a mutually beneficial arrangement was found, established between the Spanish ruler, on the one hand, and the rabbis being in charge of the Jewish ghettos. Now, the life in the ghettos was almost completely under rabbinical control, not unlike the control that Islamic ayatollahs exercise over their population. To make money was permitted. To make money outside of the ghettos was permitted, but only in order to support Talmudic studies. And in order to do so, the Jews became the tools of the rulers, frequently in the suppression of the indigenous population. That was, in particular, the case in places like Poland and Russia. Jews working outside of the ghetto were used by the rulers as tax collectors vis-à-vis the Polish and Russian populations. The Jews were permitted to do this because... Max Weber refers to them as having a double ethic. That is, they had rules that applied to them internally that were different from the rules that applied to them externally. To give you just one example: while the Christians, for a long time, outlawed the charging of interest, the Jews also outlawed taking interest except from Christians. It was not permitted to take interest from other Jews, but it was permitted to take interest from Christians, which of course, made them particularly suitable for certain types of professions, like moneylenders.

In the ghettos—I'll give you some quotes on that in a second—the reading of books in modern languages was completely outlawed. There was no writing allowed, even in Hebrew, unless it was explicitly permitted by the rabbis. We are nowadays used to the fact that Jews are particularly humorous people. Just think of Woody Allen or Murray Rothbard. But humor was something that was considered to be taboo in the ghettos. There was rigorous enforcement of eating and sexual taboos. Education was concerned exclusively with the Talmud and mystic writings. No math was taught, no science, no history, no geography. All violations were severely punished, up to and including flogging to death. And, as I said regarding the liberation of the Jews, from that point on we see that the dramatic achievements that they were capable of was essentially a Christian achievement, due to the attachment of the puritanical values of the Old Testament, which was also part of the tradition of Judaism. As soon as they were emancipated, combine that with the puritanical attitude that they had, they then became indeed enormously successful businessmen, as successful as any other group. I want to read you a little quote on this atmosphere in the Jewish ghettos.

> [Before emancipation] there were no Jewish comedies, just as there were no comedies in Sparta, and for similar reasons. Or take the love of learning. Except for purely religious learning, which was, itself, in a debased and degenerate state. The Jews of Europe (and to a lesser extent also of the Arab countries) were dominated by a supreme contempt and hatred for all learning (excepting the Talmud and Jewish mysticism). Large parts of the Old Testament, all non-liturgical Hebrew poetry, most books on Jewish philosophy were not read and their very names were often anathematized. Study of all languages was strictly forbidden, as was the study of mathematics and science. Geography, history, even Jewish history, were completely unknown. Nothing was so forbidden, feared and therefore persecuted, as the most modest innovation or the most innocent criticism.
>
> It was a world sunk in the most abject superstition, fanaticism and ignorance, a world in which the preface to the first work on geography in Hebrew, published

> 1803 in Russia, could complain that very many great rabbis were denying the existence of the American continent and saying that it is "impossible."[8]

The Jewish contribution begins after the emancipation of the Jews, basically from the outside. Before that they do not play a dominant role in the development of capitalism, but can actually be regarded as in some ways hampering that development.

Now I come to Christianity. While Western civilization eventually came to surpass all other civilizations, one has to admit that this was nothing that was obvious from the very beginning. Early Christianity was not individualistic, but it was absorbed in the collective community, to which a person was rigidly subordinated. Again, not quite unlike in Islam, earthly life was considered to be a mere preparation for the afterlife, and during the first millennium of influence exercised by Christianity, one must admit that Christianity presided over a regression in scientific knowledge and the division of labor. Recall, we saw this in an earlier lecture when we looked at population figures from 200 or 300 AD until about the year 1000; there is actually retrogression taking place—the population does not increase at all, and nothing in terms of scientific, scholarly, or technological achievements is accomplished during this period. So, what we have to say is that what we describe as a Western Christian outlook developed only gradually, especially through the incorporation of Greek Aristotelian ideas, culminating in Thomas Aquinas.

With Aquinas, the modern Christian view developed. Let me now describe this modern Christian view that turned out to be, obviously, quite successful in terms of the contributions that they made to science and economic development. In this modern Christian world view, the world is viewed basically as good and the greatest good lies in the future. The material and the spiritual world are seen as a unity. Recall, in Buddhism, for instance, it is somewhere suggested that the spiritual life separate itself from the flesh. In Christianity, spirit and body form a unity, and salvation also involves both, the body and the soul. There

---

[8]Israel Shahak, *Jewish History, Jewish Religion: The Weight of Three Thousand Years* (London: Pluto Press, 1994), p. 18.

exists no soul without a body and only by the performance of bodily actions can the soul be saved. Man, as I mentioned before, in the Christian world view, is considered to be the high point of creation. Man is given dominion over the world; he is clearly separated and ranks above the animal kingdom. For Christians, there exists no such thing as a golden age that is in the past. Quite the contrary, progress is possible and the future holds promises for Christians. The world and the truth is knowable, because God has withdrawn and we can discover eternal laws. Wisdom comes as a consequence of effort; it is not automatically there, but requires achievements and efforts on the part of man, and it takes time to develop.

The social world is hierarchical, to a certain extent. There is God, and the pope, and then the cardinals, the bishops and the priests, and in the earthly realm, there is a king, the Lord, the father, the mother and the child. There is no ridiculous "equality." The Christian church is antidemocratic, at least the Catholic Church is antidemocratic, but it is also individualistic, in the sense that everyone is created by God and everyone is capable of salvation, which attitude or outlook, of course, is mainly responsible for the fact that it was only in Christianity that one gradually got rid of the institution of slavery. Initially, of course, in old Christianity, slavery existed too, and there's no clear-cut prohibition against it, but based on this view that everybody is a creature of God and capable of salvation and on the attitude that Christians were a missionary religion, trying to convert people, gradually the view became the dominant view that slavery is incompatible with Christian attitudes. It was not by accident that it was a few Spanish priests who, after the occupation and conquest of South America, were responsible for, not with immediate success, obviously, but over the time, with some success, to give rise to the opinion that the Indians, after all, are also human beings and not wild creatures that should be automatic objects of enslavement.

In addition, Christianity is social and cooperative and views the progress that is possible as a result of a cooperative effort. So, it is cooperation between people that brings us closer to the truth. And I'll just make one remark about Catholicism and then I'll come to a comparison between Protestantism and Catholicism. There is, of course, one strand of Christianity that has to be regarded with some degree of suspicion when it comes to the question of how suitable it is to allow the development of capitalism and capital accumulation. That would be the extreme Paulist view that one should love *everyone* like one loves oneself, instead of taking the view that one should love one's *neighbor* as one loves oneself. It is possible to love your neighbor, but if your neighbors encompass, so to speak, the entire world and you are supposed to be charitable to the entire world, then this would, obviously, be a main obstacle in the way of capital accumulation. But, nonetheless, this is not the mainstream view, as far as I understand it.

Now, to the famous thesis of Max Weber, which you are all familiar with. Max Weber, of course, explains the rise of capitalism with the development of puritanical religions. And as we will see, there is some basic truth in this thesis, with some reservations. Now, capitalism as we know it was, of course, born in Italy and Italy is Catholic, so that clearly shows that Catholicism is definitely compatible with capitalism. In fact, the Roman church was a major banking institution, that is, it represented itself as a capitalist institution. And the first big centers of capitalism were Florence and Venice, again, Catholic places. And in addition one can say that as a matter of theology, Catholicism is, of course, far more enthusiastic about human existence and human autonomy and human reason and human intellect than, let's say, Lutheranism and Calvinism is. Lutheranism and Calvinism are anti-intellectual doctrines, to a certain extent. For the Thomist, faith and intellect can somehow be reconciled and combined. For Lutherans and Calvinists, there exists a strict separation between the two, and they emphasize far more the importance of faith, of blind faith, than they emphasize reason.

On the other hand, in the Catholic religion, you have, of course, a greater emphasis on the enjoyment of life and you have, relatively speaking, a certain disdain for material things, that would, relating to the previous lecture, indicate that Catholics tend to have a slightly higher degree of time preference. And again, in looking at the present world, you can somehow see that that is true. I mean, *la dolce vita*—the good life or the sweet life—is something that is typical of southern countries, of Italy and Spain. *La dolce vita* in Germany in the nineteenth century was more or less unheard of. In the meantime, of course, we all live in some sort of secular age, so the Germans also do *dolce vita* plenty, in the meantime. But, again, talking about the time of a few hundred years ago when capitalism developed, it's certainly clear that there was more of, as Murray Rothbard would say, life-affirming attitude among the Catholics, than there was among the Protestants for whom life was something less than enjoyable, to put it mildly.

In the twentieth century, I'm not sure if it applies anymore, but it seems to be that everybody has fun all the time, but in the old days, I think Catholics definitely had more fun because your sins could be easily forgiven, whereas the sins, of course, they stick with a Protestant forever. They never get rid of them. In fact, private property, until 1891, when Pope Leo XIII declared private property to be a good, private property had, before, been seen by the Catholics, as a regrettable, though unavoidable concession to the weakness of human nature. They were not opposed to it, but they thought it had something to do with human weakness and one had, regrettably, to accept this institution. Only relatively late, with Leo XIII, as a positive affirmation, was private property seen as a good thing.

Nonetheless, despite this more rationalistic attitude among Catholics, as compared to the blind faith attitude found among Protestants, Weber seems to be fundamentally right in the following way. In mixed populations, like in France or Germany, where large parts of the population are Catholic and large parts are Protestant, and Germany is almost half and half, we do find a significant overrepresentation of Protestants among the capitalists, and in general we can say that of course, capitalism was further developed and was more successful in northern Europe and also in the United States, than in southern Europe. And, of course, northern Europe is predominantly Protestant. This cannot be explained with the interest question. That is, Protestants had less difficulties with charging interest than Catholics, but in the Catholic doctrine, the interest prohibition had been by and large, undermined completely at the time. So, this is likely not the explanation for the greater success, as far as capitalistic development is concerned, of Protestant places.

Certainly, the doctrine of predestination has nothing to do with the greater success of the Protestant religions. If anything, if people had taken the doctrine of predestination seriously, they would have fallen into some kind of Oriental lethargic fatalism. After all, if all is predestined, why should I do anything? So, what we can infer from this is that the doctrine of predestination, while it existed on the books, was never really taken seriously by anybody. What is the most likely explanation for the greater amount of capital accumulation and success and so forth, of the Protestant religion, is simply their puritanical outlook, which involves the idea that you work without enjoyment. Work is the only way to riches. The riches or wealth that you accumulate are an indicator of grace. Work is, for Protestants, almost like prayer. There's a certain amount of asceticism that Protestants accept. You don't enjoy life; you just pain yourself, work harder and harder.

There is, among the Protestants, a more pronounced rejection of ostentatious consumption and of ostentatious displays of wealth. Again, you can see that even now; the rich people in countries like Italy or Spain live in places that look like rich people live there. I know many rich people in Germany that live in places which look no different from the place where I live. There is a rejection, of course, of gambling among the Puritans, drinking, all the rest of it. All of this that we might regard as an achievement of the puritanical religions, Lutheranism and Calvinism, however, might be regarded as some sort of mixed blessing, because what was truly unique in the Western world, and might have had a far greater impact on the ultimate superiority of Western civilization as compared to others than the Christian religion itself, is the fact that only in Europe was the power of the church and the power of the earthly rulers institutionally separated.

You had the pope in Rome, the Catholic Church being an international church, counterbalancing the power of the various local lords, reducing the power of these lords because they did not control the church at the same time. But, this separation of church and state, which was unique for Europe and existed in no other part of the world, this unique separation was, of course, to a large extent, if not completely, broken up and abolished, precisely through the Protestant Revolution. That is, by breaking up the international Catholic Church and founding various national churches—Lutherans, Calvinists, and Mr. Knox in Scotland and so forth—all of a sudden, the princely rulers realized that this gives the possibility for me to combine the highest rank in the worldly hierarchy, as king or prince, with the highest rank also in the church.

And insofar as—and this is the mixed blessing—Protestantism has systematically strengthened the power of the state and Protestantism has also been responsible, to a large extent, for the promotion of democratic values. Remember, I explained that in the Catholic Church you have hierarchies. The Catholic Church is in this sense antidemocratic. The Protestant churches are far more democratic. The high churches, the high Protestant churches have gone back, to a certain extent, in the direction of the Catholic Church because they were aware of the dangers that result if you let every individual interpret the Bible on his own. If you do that and if you have a document that is not internally consistent, then you get a splitting off of all sorts of weird sects. This is, of course, precisely, what one of the side effects of the Protestant Revolution was, that you had a multiplication of weird people, of weird things happening all of a sudden, which happens, of course, if every individual just interprets whatever he thinks is right, and nothing is filtered through some people who have more wisdom than others. And of course, the Lutheran Church, which was initially quite democratic, has abolished this, has also built up hierarchies, though not to the same extent as the Catholic Church, and so has the Anglican Church. And if you look at the present situation, the craziest churches are, of course, the churches that are most democratic, up to this point.

I want to briefly touch upon a very politically sensitive, if not to say, dangerous, subject. Again, I must say, I dared to bring it up at my university and I have not yet received any complaints. This is a table that is culled from *IQ and the Wealth of Nations,* a book recently published by Richard Lynn and Tatu Vanhanen, who did some very simple and elementary investigation and what they did was to try to show whether there exists some sort of correlation between IQ and measures of economic output such as GNP, or not.

I should say from the outset that they did not just use one IQ measure for countries; they typically had, from most of the countries, several types of IQ measures available. They showed first that these measures are all highly intercorrelated, convincing us that we can put a certain amount of trust in the numbers that they use, and they also did not just use one economic output measure such as GNP, but also if it was available, two or three, and again intercorrelated them and tried to show that there was a high internal consistency among the numbers. Now, the correlation that they established—and I'll say something about the interpretation of this table—is extremely high for social sciences. It is close to 0.7, which is, if you have ever done empirical research in sociology or psychology or so, mind-bogglingly high. I mean, people are usually impressed already if you have correlations of 0.2 or 0.3 or something like that. That is already considered to be worth showing. So here, we get very high correlations.

The interpretation of Table 1 follows simply from the heading. The first number refers to the IQ; the second number is the actual GDP per capita in the year 1998, and the third number is called Fitted GDP, which would be the calculated GDP based on a regression analysis; that is, what we should expect the GDP to be, given the IQ in that country and taking the stable relationship between IQ and GDP into

Table 1
The Results of the Regression Analysis in Which Real GDP Per Capita 1998 is Used as the Dependent Variable and National IQ is Used as the Independent Variable for 81 Countries

Country	IQ	Real GDP per capita 1998	Residual Real GDP	Fitted Real GDP
Argentina	96	12,013	-2,094	14,107
Australia	98	22,452	7,307	15,145
Austria	102	23,166	5,945	17,221
Barbados	78	12,001	7,236	4,765
Belgium	100	23,223	7,040	16,183
Brazil	87	6,625	-2,811	9,436
Bulgaria	93	4,809	-7,741	12,550
Canada	97	23,582	8,956	14,626
China	100	3,105	-13,078	16,183
Colombia	89	6,006	-4,468	10,474
Congo (Brazzaville)	73	995	-1,175	2,170
Congo (Zaire)	65	822	2,804	-1,982
Croatia	90	6,749	-4,244	10,993
Cuba	85	3,967	-4,431	8,398
Czech. Republic	97	12,362	-2,264	14,626
Denmark	98	24,218	9,073	15,145

Reproduced from Richard Lynn and Tatu Vanhanen, *IQ and the Wealth of Nations* (Westport, CT: Praeger, 2002), pp. 100–03.

Country	IQ	Real GDP per capita 1998	Residual Real GDP	Fitted Real GDP
Ecuador	80	3,003	-2,800	5,803
Egypt	83	3,041	-4,319	7,360
Equatorial Guinea	59	1,817	6,913	-5,096
Ethiopia	63	574	3,594	-3,020
Fiji	84	4,231	-3,648	7,879
Finland	97	20,847	6,221	14,626
France	98	21,175	6,030	15,145
Germany	102	22,169	4,948	17,221
Ghana	71	1,735	603	1,132
Greece	92	13,943	1,912	12,031
Guatemala	79	3,505	-1,779	5,284
Guinea	66	1,782	3,245	-1,463
Hong Kong	107	20,763	946	19,817
Hungary	99	10,232	-5,432	15,664
India	81	2,077	-4,245	6,322
Indonesia	89	2,651	-7,823	10,474
Iran	84	5,121	-2,758	7,879
Iraq	87	3,197	-6,239	9,436
Ireland	93	21,482	8,932	12,550
Israel	94	17,301	4,232	13,069
Italy	102	20,585	3,364	17,221
Jamaica	72	3,389	1,738	1,651
Japan	105	23,257	4,478	18,779
Kenya	72	980	-671	1,651
Korea, South	106	13,478	-5,820	19,298
Lebanon	86	4,326	-4,591	8,917
Malaysia	92	8,137	-3,894	12,031
Marshall Islands	84	3,000	-4,879	7,879
Mexico	87	7,704	-1,732	9,436
Morocco	85	3,305	-5,093	8,398
Nepal	78	1,157	-3,608	4,765
Netherlands	102	22,176	4,955	17,221
New Zealand	100	17,288	1,105	16,183

Country	IQ	Real GDP per capita 1998	Residual Real GDP	Fitted Real GDP
Nigeria	67	795	1,739	-944
Norway	98	26,342	11,197	15,145
Peru	90	4,282	-6,711	10,993
Philippines	86	3,555	-5,362	8,917
Poland	99	7,619	-8,045	15,664
Portugal	95	14,701	1,113	13,589
Puerto Rico	84	8,000	121	7,879
Qatar	78	20,987	16,222	4,765
Romania	94	5,648	-7,421	13,069
Russia	96	6,460	-7,647	14,107
Samoa (Western)	87	3,832	-5,604	9,436
Sierra Leone	64	458	2,959	-2,501
Singapore	103	24,210	6,470	17,740
Slovakia	96	9,699	-4,408	14,107
Slovenia	95	14,293	705	13,588
South Africa	72	8,488	6,837	1,651
Spain	97	16,212	1,586	14,626
Sudan	72	1,394	-257	1,651
Suriname	89	5,161	-5,313	10,474
Sweden	101	20,659	3,957	16,702
Switzerland	101	25,512	8,810	16,702
Taiwan	104	13,000	-5,260	18,260
Tanzania	72	480	-1,171	1,651
Thailand	91	5,456	-6,056	11,512
Tonga	87	3,000	-6,436	9,436
Turkey	90	6,422	-4,571	10,993
Uganda	73	1,074	-1,096	2,170
United Kingdom	100	20,336	4,153	16,183
United States	98	29,605	14,460	15,145
Uruguay	96	8,623	-5,484	14,107
Zambia	77	719	-3,527	4,246
Zimbabwe	66	2,669	4,132	-1,463

consideration. The countries are ordered here in alphabetical order, all the way to Zimbabwe.

I should make one remark about the more underdeveloped countries. In the more underdeveloped countries, the actual GDP tends to be underestimated, because in very highly agricultural societies, where there is a relatively high degree of self-sufficiency, GDP numbers understate the productive output because GDP measures only goods and services that were actually bought and sold in markets. So, if you grow your own tomatoes and your own potatoes, they would not be counted, whereas if you grow potatoes and tomatoes and then sell them on the market, then they would be counted. Obviously, in terms of standard of living, that would make no difference, but in terms of GDP or GNP, numbers such as this, in one case it would be counted and in the other case it would not be counted.

The overall impression that you get from this list is that those countries that have high IQs also have high GDPs. And those countries that have very low IQs have, on the average, very low GDPs. There are, however, some clear-cut exceptions, obviously, which would have to be explained differently. Take the case of China, which is here listed with an IQ of 100 and a GDP per capita of $3,000 and a calculated GDP of $16,000. Now here, the explanation is that China was and still is, to a certain extent, a Communist country, leading, of course, to extremely low actual GDP and leading us, on the other hand, to the conclusion that if this type of system were abolished, the potential of China is significant. That is, we can expect GDPs of $16,000 per person or in the neighborhood of that. There are also some countries that seem to be overperforming. The Germans produce a higher GDP than their IQ would indicate, for instance. The same is true for the US, if I remember correctly. The US has an IQ of 98, and it has a significantly higher actual GDP than predicted GDP based on the intelligence of the population, which again, we would explain with having a relatively freer market system than some other places have. One might object to a table such as this, "Doesn't intelligence also have something to do with picking the right economic system?" So, maybe there is something wrong with the Chinese, despite having such a great potential; after all, for a considerable amount of time, they lagged behind to such a great extent.

We can also—again, I do not want to overinterpret this table—but, you can also see, for instance, how relatively vain the attempt is, for instance, to expect economic miracles in Africa to take place. If you look at African countries and look at the IQs there, you will have a rather dim impression as far as the growth potential of those countries are concerned.

I will end this discussion—I think the table itself is highly interesting to study—by saying that, of course, IQs are also not what we might call invariable biological constants. They are subject to variation as well, even though it is not as easy to vary them as many other things. Obviously, we would expect that the old Babylonians and the old Egyptians must have done somewhat better than the present-day Babylonians and the present-day Egyptians, given their relatively low performance nowadays and their glorious achievements in the past. The most straightforward way to imagine that these numbers are subject to influence is to just realize that populations can, of course, engage in eugenic breeding practices, so to speak. For instance, societies where the upper classes, the more intelligent people, have it as a habit to have larger numbers of children, and the lower classes with lower IQs have smaller numbers of children, that would lead, over a few generations, obviously, to an upward lifting of average IQs. The same thing, of course, also applies in reverse. That is, if you had the lower classes with lower IQ levels producing the overwhelming bulk of children, and the upper classes producing very few or none, then one would expect that over the timespan of several generations the average IQ would fall.

Hypotheses have been advanced, for instance, for why is it that Jews tend to have a very high IQ, even though Israel here is not particularly outstanding, with an IQ of 94, but the Jewish population in the United States has an IQ well above. Partially, that can be explained simply by migration. That is, the more successful people are more mobile and go to places where there is more opportunity for them, and there is a larger concentration of those. For instance, they have done studies where they compare the IQ of Scots who live in London as compared with Scots who remain in Scotland and found that the IQ of Scots in London was significantly higher than Scots who stayed behind in Scotland. Again, that has a rather obvious explanation: the smarter ones moved. The case of East Germany versus West Germany is also interesting. They do not break it up here; German is simply listed as IQ of 102, but I have seen comparisons between East Germany and West Germany, and there the difference was that West Germany had one of 104 and East Germany of 98. And again, there exists a very straightforward explanation for a phenomenon such as this. East Germany was under socialist rule and expropriated the property of most of the successful individuals, and the most successful individuals left the country. So, of course, that lifted the IQ in West Germany and lowered the IQ in East Germany. Another explanation that has been advanced, coming back to the case of the Jews, for instance—I tend to be somewhat skeptical about that one, but just for illustrative purposes, I might mention it—that the largest numbers of children were in Orthodox Jewish families, typically produced by rabbis. If one assumes that the rabbis were the smartest of the bunch, then you would expect an upward tendency in IQs simply by a different type of breeding behavior. Clearly, explanations along this line are not sufficient when it comes to explaining the wealth of nations, but I think one would also be blind to the facts, if one simply dismisses things like this easily. The evidence that Lynn and Vanhanen present is dramatic and overwhelming. You will be shocked to see how easy the explanation for a phenomenon can be sometimes, an explanation that other people struggle around for decades and do not explain.

LECTURE 6

The Production of Law and Order, Natural Order, Feudalism, and Federalism

---

THE TOPIC OF THIS LECTURE is the production of law and order within a natural order. That is, the production of law and order without a state. Tomorrow, I will talk about the origin of the state, but here we are still considering what would naturally evolve; just as the division of labor naturally evolves, money as a medium of exchange naturally evolves, capital accumulation will take place under decently favorable circumstances and not so much under less favorable circumstances, so it can also be expected that every society will develop mechanisms for defending itself against asocial individuals. As long as mankind is what it is, we will have people who engage in productive activities and never have any other desire but to be productive individuals. So long as that is the case, we will also have people who try to hit other people on the head and rob and rape them, and every society that wants to survive will have to do something about this.

I will first return briefly to the subject of property and property rights, because what it is that we want to defend in a natural order is, of course, property and the rights of people to their property. We have seen that people take it for granted, even from the very most primitive situation on, that they own themselves, due to the direct connection that we have with our physical bodies. People also never had any doubt that those tools that they themselves produced were their tools and not somebody else's tools. When it came to the development of settled agriculture, this idea was expanded to pieces of land. People then began to put up signs in order to claim certain plots of land as theirs, and these signs typically consisted in visibly doing something to the land so that other people could see that this is not a piece of uncultivated wilderness, but rather that this is a piece of land that has been worked on. Somebody has done something to it, and I can see that. And as you will admit, of course, it is quite easy in almost all cases to distinguish between a piece of land that has been cultivated in any way by mankind and a piece of wilderness. Just drive through, say, the Rocky Mountains, and you will see that most of the places are completely untouched, nobody has done anything to them and you can see that that is the case. On the other hand, drive through similar mountain ranges in Europe, let's say in Austria and Switzerland. You see that people have, indeed, cultivated the mountains all the way to the top of the mountain. That is visible for anyone who has eyes to see. And, of course, people will show willingness to defend themselves against invaders trying to take these cultivated pieces of land away from them.

Let me emphasize again why it is that we need norms of property. If goods are scarce, then conflicts over these goods are possible. If we want to avoid conflicts over the use of scarce resources, there exists only one method to do it, and that is to formulate rules of exclusive use regarding scarce resources. That is, formulating rules that say that one person can do something with it, but others are excluded from it. As long as all of us have access to the scarce resources, conflicts are unavoidable. As a result, we can say that property norms, in this sense, are natural and necessary institutions for avoiding conflicts. And the rule of the first one to produce something, the first one to appropriate something, is that he becomes the owner and not somebody else (such as the second one or the third one or the rest of mankind sharing in what somebody else has originally appropriated). You can recognize the naturalness of this rule by recognizing that if mankind wants to act without conflicts, from the beginning of mankind on, then, the rule that the first one to use something becomes the owner of it is the only rule that makes this possible—that is, that mankind can, from the beginning of mankind on, conceivably act without any conflicts. In this sense, these norms are natural norms or natural laws. No other laws have this advantage of making it possible to avoid conflicts between humans from the very beginning of mankind on.

There's only one additional consideration that I want to present when it comes to conflicts over property rights, and that concerns the problem of *easements*. So, if this is my piece of land and I have no neighbor so far and I spew out smoke here, there, and everywhere, and after a while, somebody settles next to me, can this person (B) complain about person A (me, the original settler) that he causes physical damage to the property of B? And the answer is no, in this case, he can't, because person A has acquired what is called an easement. He was there first and nobody's property was damaged by his initial activities. If somebody else now comes along, B, then what B has appropriated is, from the outset, *soiled or dirty property*. And if B wants to have *unsoiled or clean property*, then B must pay A to stop this. But, A, being there first, has acquired an easement to continue with this activity if he so desires. B must pay A in order to stop it.

If the situation is the other way around, that is, B is here first and then A settles next to B and then spews out his smoke or whatever it is, onto B's property, then the situation is different. B has acquired clean property, and he has acquired an easement for his property to be left clean. In this case, he could take out an injunction against A and tell A that you must stop this or you must pay me in order for me to let you continue with this activity. These are the elementary rules that have been accepted by mankind for thousands of years. Again, there exist disputes sometimes about who was there first and who was there second, but those rules were considered to be the basic fundamental rules of dealing with conflicts arising over who owns what and who is permitted to do what and who is not permitted to do what. When we are talking about the production of security in a natural order, I have in mind the defense of these principles. Who has appropriated something first, has the right to defend it. Who was there first, without any neighbors, acquires an easement if certain negative externalities result, or if negative externalities come later, then the initial owner has the right to stop these negative externalities.

Now, in a natural order, the first thing that I want to point out, is that this does not only include self-defense. I've already mentioned the fact that insofar as we control something, we automatically would defend ourselves against people who try to take control away over things that we ourselves are in control of. We also, from the very beginning, select the places where we have our property, partly with consideration of how easy or difficult these things are to defend where they are. To just give you an example, the location of Venice is somehow in the marshes, but it is difficult for invaders, especially in an age when you had very limited technological abilities, to invade a place like this because you have to go through the water and the water is flat and you don't know your way around; it is easier to defend a place like this. So, the location of many places was chosen precisely with this idea in mind. Is it a place that can be easily defended? Of course, if there's nobody around for tens of thousands of miles, you are alone, then that might not be an important consideration for you to choose certain locations, but if you are surrounded by other people, then these sorts of considerations are of importance. The same thing is true for the low countries, the Netherlands. They also offer certain possibilities for defending yourself by flooding certain areas and making an invasion by land very difficult. Another example would be valleys in mountain regions. Some people settled in Swiss valleys, very remote valleys in high elevations, precisely because they knew that those were places that were comparatively easy to defend and very difficult to occupy. Even in modern times, this has made a difference. The Germans could have probably, because of their significantly larger size, invaded a country such as Switzerland, but Switzerland had, on the one hand, a militia, every man being armed and having semiautomatic machine guns at home with ammunition in the closet.[1] And also, of course, because a country like Switzerland is very difficult to invade and occupy because of its mountainous terrain. You can see that, again, how our brave

[1]I still remember how impressed my children were when I took them to one of my Swiss friends and then he opened the closet and there was a big gun and enough ammunition to kill half of the German population.

soldiers in Afghanistan struggle up and down the mountains to find the people that they are looking for. Or take a place like San Marino, which sits on top of a 1,000-foot mountain with a big fortress around, and a population of 8,000 people; they were able to defend themselves for 1,500 years from any invasion.

The second thing I want to point out is the way justice will be done in small societies. We always hear about the necessity of having a state, in order to do justice. The world provides us with hundreds of thousands of examples of how absolutely ludicrous this idea is. In every little society encompassing a few people, there are very quickly a few people rising to the rank of some sort of authority. They are braver, smarter, more successful, more trusted than others. You can see that in every village. And whenever there is a conflict, that is, A steals something from B or A knocks over B and they fight over who did it and who didn't do it, while it was possible that they engaged in vigilante justice, that is, tried to beat the crap out of each other right on the spot, in most cases and for good reasons, they don't do that because it is very difficult, then, to justify themselves afterward before the other members of the village. So, they turn to people who have more authority than others do and these people, let's call them nobles, or aristocrats, or the elite, whatever the term is, it doesn't matter—these people will then act as judge, typically without charging any fee, just out of the responsibility of being a leader of a small community. And based on their judgment and on their authority that they have among their fellow men, this judgment then will be enforced automatically. In most cases, there's not even violence necessary in order to enforce it on the person who was found to be guilty. The person himself will accept it and will be willing to provide restitution, because otherwise he will be expelled from the community; he will be an outcast and nothing is, in those societies, worse than being an outcast. Again, even in modern times, this sort of ostracism works magnificently in many professions.

I met a large grain dealer in Switzerland at some point. He had dealings with grain dealers all over the world, and he reported that they had a dispute regarding certain qualities of grains and delayed deliveries from a grain dealer in the Soviet Union. This was at the time when the Soviet Union was still intact. No regular court was involved, just the association of grain dealers handled this. The proceedings took place in the Soviet Union, and the unanimous verdict was that the guy in the Soviet Union had done wrong. The judgment was enforced and this person was thrown out of this association of merchant dealers, of grain dealers. Nobody dealing in grain would have anything to do with this person ever again. Mere ostracism was entirely sufficient to do it.

Now, of course, you sometimes have recalcitrant people, people who were by and large forced to give compensation to the victim. That was a principle of punishment, to provide compensation to the victim. You realize, of course, that criminals nowadays do not compensate their victims at all. As a matter of fact, victims typically have to shell out more money so that recalcitrant criminals can play table tennis, watch TV, engage in workouts, get their müesli and whatever it is in prison. A very different situation than what would exist in a natural order. But, even on this relatively primitive level, we would, of course, expect that there are certain limitations to self-defense, and that people would want to rely on specialized defense providers. They want to take advantage of the division of labor also in this field. Not everybody is equally good at protecting somebody else. That's why bars usually have big people standing in front of the door making sure who goes in and who doesn't go in, and not teeny old ladies. So, yes, division of labor is as important in that area as it is in others.

And what I want to do now is first to describe how this system of defending oneself against aggressors worked during the feudal times, during the Middle Ages, a time when no state existed, just a large number of highly decentralized lords and vassals, etc. And then, in the next step, I will explain with some cues taken from the feudal order how such a system would work in modern times.

Now, in these feudal times, there existed landlords, owners of pieces of land, and they had tenants, tenant-farmers. Both were contractually connected. Most of the stuff that we learn about feudalism tends to be half-truths at best. Feudalism has a very bad name, an undeservedly bad name. The contract between the landlords and the tenants typically provided for the landlord providing protection and the tenant working for a certain period of time for the landlord, and in cases of conflict, the tenant is also willing and prepared to fight on the side of the landlord. Law was at that time considered something that was given. Law was not considered to be something that was made by people, but something that existed eternally and was just simply discovered. People learned what it was. New law was from the very outset considered to be suspicious, because law had to be old, it had to be something that had always existed. Anybody who came up with some sort of new law, was automatically dismissed as probably a fraud. The subjects, the tenants, had a right to resist. That is, they were not subject to their lords no matter what, because, as I said, there existed an eternally valid law, which protected the tenant as much as the landlord, and if the landlord did break this law, then the tenants had the right to resist, up to the point of killing the landlord.

Landlords, in turn, had been contractually tied to other landlords. The lords had, so to speak, other overlords and again, these contracts provided by and large for mutual assistance agreements. If such and such happens, you will provide so-and-so many soldiers who are peasants to do this and you do such and such and so forth. And what came about was called the feudal pyramid. That is, another contract with somebody who might be even more powerful, meaning, in this case, someone who had even larger landholdings and a larger number of tenants, all the way up to the king. Not only that, people frequently had contracts with various lords, with competing lords, so to speak, as some sort of insurance policy. That is, if this guy does something to me, I also have another protector. And, in combination with these sorts of multiple alliances that existed, they typically agreed that if it were to come to a conflict between the two lords to which they had pledged their allegiance, then they would remain neutral. Peasants who were not associated directly with any particular lord in some sort of protection agreement, isolated peasants, usually chose the king as their protector. That is, someone slightly more removed, but they also received some sort of legal protection by associating themselves with the king directly.

There existed also so-called *allodial owners*, that is, people who were big landowners in their own right and who had no allegiances to anyone, and would meet the king on an even level so to speak. They might have less land than the king had, and fewer tenants and fewer soldiers working for them, but in dealings with the king they were his equals. The lords, on their territory, had complete jurisdiction over their territory, including over all those people who lived on that territory. That is, they were the judges over their own peasants, their warriors, their house personnel, etc. Intervening into the internal affairs of a lord was not permitted. In this sense, they had a similar status that, let's say, embassies have nowadays, where the United States cannot simply go into the Embassy of China and then do whatever they want. In the Chinese Embassy, the Chinese rule themselves. The lords were in charge of their dominion, and they represented their tenants or vassals in external affairs. The king was typically a person who came from a particularly noble family, a family that was recognized as a family of great achievement, and was always chosen from this family, but was not hereditary in the sense that it was perfectly clear who would become the next king. It was all the other nobles, who were contractually connected with each other, who determined unanimously which of the members of the king's family should become king.

Eventually, this type of principle that combined hereditary elements with elective elements disappeared, and either the hereditary element took over or the pure elective element took over. But in the initial states, it was a combination of these two elements, the king coming always out of the same family, but who from this family would become the king depended on the result of an election among the lords. These assemblies of lords that selected the king became, in a way, the precursors of what we today consider to be parliaments. But, of course, only nobles, that is, landlords themselves, not tenants, were in charge of electing the king.

The king's main task consisted, with the agreement of his assembled nobles, in declaring cases of emergency, war or something like this, but only with the unanimous consent of the nobles assembled in this parliament. And, in addition, the king had the function of some sort of appeals court, that people who thought that injustice had been committed against them, including an injustice by their own lord, could appeal to the king for final justice. The early feudal kings traveled around frequently from town to town. They were sort of the wandering judges. There existed no such thing as capital cities. In the German case, for instance, there were places where regular court sessions were held, in Nierenberg, in Augsburg, in Ladenburg, in Frankfurt, in Prague, in Vienna and several other places. All of these places had an elevated status as places where one could seek justice, but no capital existed.

Also, the king could not tax. Taxes, in the modern sense, did not exist. The king lived off his own estate, just as all lords lived off their own estates. All that he could do in cases of war was to go to his various nobles and beg them, give me a little bit, whereby every noble was perfectly entitled to say no and nothing would happen to him. The task of the king was also, in addition, with the agreement of the nobles, to decide about cases of war, to establish on the outskirts of these loose associations of lords and nobles, so-called protection villages, where people were settled, selected due to their particular abilities as fighters, in order to protect, let's say, Christendom from the Turks or something like this. They were called *WereDörfer* or fortified villages, especially because their task assisted in the defense against societies that were considered to be outside the society that was combined or integrated through these intricate systems of feudal contract relationships.

Not only did the right to resistance exist among the tenants against their landlords, very importantly, it was also possible that these tenants, if they felt oppressed by their landlord, could run away and simply associate and get protection from a neighboring lord, which was, of course, the best protection that you can have from being oppressed in the first place, knowing that all you have to do is run away and attach yourself to some other protector and thereby get rid of your previous lord. On this point, in particular, that is, the ability of people to run away and attach themselves to a different protector, I want to quote Herbert Spencer, who describes the situation in ancient Rome, which was very similar in its feudal structure to Europe during the Middle Ages. Rome was also a famous place for complete dominion of the master of the household over his tenants and servants, including his children and wife. Herbert Spencer writes about early Rome,

> [W]hile coercive rule within the family and the group of related families was easy, there was difficulty in extending coercion over many such groups; fortified as they were [and again, these feudal landlords, of course, all had certain amounts of fortifications] against one another. Moreover, the stringency of government within each of the communities [that is, each of the clans,] constituting the primitive city, was diminished by facility of escape from one and admission into

> another. As we have seen among simple tribes, desertions take place when the rule is harsh; and we may infer that, in primitive Rome there was a check on exercise of force by the more powerful families in each settlement over the less powerful, caused by the fear that migration might weaken the settlement and strengthen an adjacent one. Thus the circumstances were such that when, for defense of the city, cooperation became needful, the heads of the clans included in its several divisions came to have substantially equal powers. The original senate was the collective body of clan elders; and "this assembly of elders was the ultimate holder of the ruling power:" it was "an assembly of Kings."[2]

Now, let me emphasize this point again. Just as important for the successful development of Western Europe was the fact that there was separation between church and state, which was different from all other regions on the globe. So it was of utmost importance for the dynamic development of Western Europe that Western Europe was a political anarchy, that is to say, thousands of independent landlord nobles somehow connected together through contracts, but each being his own man, and the ease with which people could move from one jurisdiction to another, which tends to contribute, of course, to moderation on the part of each one of these rulers. Each one must be afraid that if I'm too draconian in my punishment of my own men, then they will attach themselves to somebody else and strengthen people who, in some situations, might become my enemy. In addition, one more element should be mentioned in order to characterize the feudal world, and that is the existence of cities. And these cities were typically founded either by bishops or by nobles, by lords or by associations of merchants and in some cases, of course, also by—as in the case of Switzerland, for instance—by *Eidgenossenschaften*, "oath fellowships" or confederations.

---

[2]Herbert Spencer, *Principles of Sociology*, 2d ed. (New York: D. Appleton Co., 1916), vol. 2, pp. 378–79.

This is the structure that the initial founding cantons in Switzerland had, where all free men swore an oath that they would come to mutually assist each other in case of an attack against them. And these cities frequently had written law codes, that is, Magdeburg Law or Hamburg Law or Hanover Law or Lübeck Law, etc., so that people who moved to these cities knew what law code would apply to them, and when new cities were founded, the normal thing to do was to adopt one of the already existing law codes and maybe make a few amendments to it. That is, some law codes became the law codes, not just of one city, but of many, many cities, who adopted the initial example of a place that first took the initiative to write these laws down.

In this connection, let me make a little side remark. In English-speaking countries, America and England, there is a certain amount of pride in having the so-called common law, which is, in a way, noncodified law, or case law. The Continental tradition, as you know, has been for a long time different. There, we have had codified law taken from the Romans, especially from the East Romans who had codified this law for the first time in an extensive manner and then, of course, in modern times, the Napoleonic Code, which has been taken over by most Continental European states in one form or another with some modifications. And, as I said, Anglo-Saxons looked down on codified law and hailed their own noncodified common law. I want to just remark that, for instance, Max Weber has a very interesting observation regarding this. He sees the reason for the noncodification of the common law in the self-interest of the lawyers to make the law difficult to understand for the layman and thus make a lot of money. He emphasizes that codified law makes it possible for the layman on the street who can read to study the law book himself and go to court himself and point out, here, that this law is written down. So, maybe this excessive pride that the Anglo-Saxons have in their common law might be a little bit overdrawn.

In terms of punishment, as I said, compensation to the victim was the main principle; some system of paying fines for various types of offenses was worked out relatively quickly. And by and large, they accepted the principle of proportionality. If you killed somebody, then you had to pay more than if you cut off somebody's arm. If you cut off somebody's arm, the fine that was imposed on you was higher than if you cut off somebody's toe, and so forth, but most of the punishments were indeed in the form of fines, either monetary fines or fines in the form of natural goods.

So now I should come to the modern world. Obviously, we cannot go back to this feudal system. My purpose was only to show that we do have historical examples where societies have developed relatively effective means of protecting themselves through systems of alliances. In the modern world, we would expect, of course, a slightly different setup and this setup would be composed mostly of three institutional devices. On the one hand, commercial insurance companies. On the other hand, freely financed police forces and freely financed arbitration and judging agencies. We can imagine that these three institutions would operate separately from each other, but be contractually aligned with the others, or we can imagine that these three institutions would be vertically integrated. That is to say, an insurance company could also have a police division and a judge division attached to it. It doesn't really matter whether it is vertically integrated or we have independent institutions. The decisive element here would be, again, that the relationships between all of these institutions would be contractual and voluntary, similar to the situation that existed during the feudal era. And I want to explain, in particular, that through such a setup, we would gradually create something like the unification of law, just as the world becomes unified through one money, and the world becomes unified through a worldwide division of labor, so the world would also become integrated through a set of universal standards of law.

Now, how would this happen? I think the main impulse in that direction would come from the insurance companies. All institutions in the modern world, all firms, all companies, everybody having an enterprise, requires insurance. To operate without insurance is almost impossible in the modern world. You can only be a very small-scale entrepreneur to do it entirely on your own, without having some sort of insurance protection. Because of this, it would not be possible, as some people have argued, that it would be the case that all institutions, all places would lay down their own peculiar rules and laws. That is, the mall has the mall laws, the school has the school laws, the steel factory has the steel factory laws. At Edward's house, the laws would be that if somebody comes in there whom he has not invited, there might be automatic shooting devices that kill the person who comes in, and things like this. Why would that not be the case? Because insurance companies would, of course, insist that many of these practices are simply not insurable. They would insist on a certain amount of uniformity of standards, which all of these insured companies (their clients) would have to adopt. They would eliminate arbitrary rules applying at this place or at that place and insist on rather general and generally known rules: on the one hand, in order to reduce general uncertainty, and on the other hand, because only if they lay down rather general rules will they be able to attract a large clientele, which is, of course, their desire.

Second, insurance companies will have inherent interest, a financial interest, in imposing on everyone who is insured by them a defensive behavioral code. The reason for this is that you can insure yourself only against risks over whose outcomes you have no personal control. I cannot insure myself, for instance, against the risk that will I provoke another person and he then smashes me in the face and then I go to my insurance company and say that he smashed me in the face and now you must defend me against him. The insurance company would say, "Look, you have to behave in an entirely defensive way, the attack must have been entirely unprovoked, only then will we defend you, but not if you have anything to do with the attack yourself." I cannot insure myself against the risk of my deliberately burning down my own house. I can insure myself against the risk that my house burns down, but no insurance company would insure me and allow me to burn down my own house and then make payment for it. So, insurance companies will insist that in order for them to cover you for any type of contingency, you have to commit yourself to a fundamentally defensive form of behavior and conduct.

By their very nature, insurance companies want to minimize damage. Minimizing the risk of damage is the business they are in; otherwise, they have to pay up. What we would get is, insurance companies might offer a certain variety in the types of contracts that they offer. One insurance company might specialize in Catholic clients and impose certain types of punishment for committing adultery for example, something that other companies would not have in their repertoire. But, they cannot be fundamentally different in the type of codes that they would offer.

Moreover, because it is now possible that conflicts arise between members of different insurance agencies, as the contracts of these different insurance companies are slightly different, whenever there are conflicts between people being insured by different insurance agencies, the only peaceful resolution that is possible is to go to an independent third-party arbitrator. These might be agencies that offer such arbitration services, and they would be independent of both insurance companies. These independent arbitration agencies are competitors, and no arbitration agency can be sure that it will be chosen again. These independent arbitration agencies obviously have an interest in not losing their clients, that is, the two conflicting insurance companies, so they develop a set of laws that can be regarded as acceptable to everyone, regardless of which particular insurance company they deal with in most cases. That is to say, these independent arbitration agencies would create, in a process of competition, something like a universally valid international law through a process of competition, and this would lead to a situation where we have a unified law structure that is valid throughout the entire world, more or less.

And this completes the process of economic and social integration: integration through the division of labor, integration through money, and integration through international law that binds all societies together, however different their internal legal structure might be. This is what I think a natural order effectively defending the property rights of individuals would look like in the modern world.

LECTURE 7

Parasitism and the Origin of the State

MY SUBJECT TODAY IS PARASITISM and the origin of the state. So far, one important element has been missing in my reconstruction of the present world. We've seen what the nature of man is, we've talked about property, the division of labor based on property, the development of money, capital accumulation, production of law and order, and the natural order resulting from all of this. Now we have to come to the disturbing elements that developed in history, those events that somehow took the natural tendencies off this path and made history deviate from its natural course.

I will begin by reminding you why we had this tendency toward a natural order. The fundamental insight was that the division of labor and human cooperation is beneficial for all people who participate in it. Division of labor implies higher productivity, and provides mankind with a reason to peacefully cooperate with each other. Otherwise, if this higher productivity associated with the division of labor did not exist, we would indeed get some sort of permanent war of each against each other. Mises writes, for instance,

> If it were not for this higher productivity of labor, based on the division of labor, men would have forever remained deadly foes of one another; irreconcilable rivals in their endeavors to secure a portion of the scarce supply of means of sustenance provided by nature. Each man would have been forced to view all other men as his enemies; his craving for the satisfaction of his own appetites would have brought him into an implacable conflict with all his neighbors. No sympathy could possibly develop under such a state of affairs.[1]

And again, because of this higher productivity, it is not necessary that people consider themselves as enemies, but can consider themselves as cooperative partners, if not even friends. And to hammer away on this point, let me once again briefly requote something that I have already quoted before, in a slightly different connection, where Mises says that

> [i]f one recognizes a principle which results in the union of all Germans...or all proletarians and forms a special nation, race or class out of individuals, then this principle cannot be proved to be effective only within the collective groups. The anti-liberal social theories [the theories that somehow emphasize that there must be conflict in humans] skim over the problem by confining themselves to the assumption that the solidarity of interests within the group is so self-evident as to be accepted without further discussion, and by taking pains only to prove the existence of the conflict of interest between groups and the necessity of conflict as the sole dynamic force of historical development. But if war is to be the father of all things, the fruitful source of historical progress, it is difficult to see why its fruitful activity should be restricted within states, nations,

[1]Ludwig von Mises, *Human Action: A Treatise on Economics*, scholar's ed. (1998; Auburn, AL: Ludwig von Mises Institute, 2008), p. 144.

> races and classes. If nature needs war, why not the war of all against all, why merely the war of all groups against all groups?[2]

Now, at this point, before I come to my genuine subject here, let me make you aware of the fact that this principle that people can cooperate peacefully with each other to their own advantage does not necessarily mean that all groups have to live in immediate neighborhood with each other. That is, even if people dislike each other, people hate each other for various other reasons, they can still peacefully cooperate with each other from some distance. That is, to accept the principle of peaceful cooperation does not at all imply the advocacy, for instance, of multicultural societies. Multicultural societies might indeed, and likely will, be extremely dangerous institutions, because people who are ethnically or culturally different do not necessarily like each other very much. But from a distance, from a physical distance, again, there is this overriding solidarity of mankind as a whole, that is, we can all benefit from each other peacefully cooperating with each other without any need to have multicultural societies anywhere on the globe.

In all of my talks so far I have concentrated, with brief deviations, on what we might call productive activities. And let me briefly explain again what I mean by productive activities, in order to distinguish productive activities from what one might call parasitic activities. Productive activities are activities that increase the well-being of at least one person, without reducing the well-being of other individuals. You realize that by this definition, we avoid all sorts of interpersonal comparisons of utility. This formulation is similar to the formulation of the so-called Pareto criterion, which also assumes that we cannot compare my happiness with your happiness. If we cannot compare your happiness with my happiness, can we still say something about social welfare increasing or not increasing? The answer is yes, we can do this if we recognize that if through my activities my well-being increases and the well-being of others is not decreased, then we can indeed say that social welfare has increased.

---

[2]Ludwig von Mises, *Socialism: An Economic and Sociological Analysis* (1951; Auburn, AL: Ludwig von Mises Institute, 2009), p. 318.

And there exist three types of activities that accomplish this, that is, making at least one person better off without making anybody else worse off: first, an act of original appropriation, that is, I am the first person to put some previously unowned resource to some use, is, in this sense, a Pareto-superior move. It makes me better off, otherwise I would not have appropriated what I appropriated, and it does not take away anything from anybody else because everybody else would have had the chance to appropriate the same thing, but they demonstrate through their own inactivity, that they did not attach sufficient value to it. So, nothing has been taken away from anybody else through an act of original appropriation, but one person is definitely better off; nobody else is made worse off as a result of it.

The second type of Pareto-superior move is to engage in acts of production. I use my own physical body, and with the help of originally appropriated resources I now transform something that was less valuable into something that I expect to be more valuable. Obviously, I am better off because of this, otherwise I would not have engaged in this act of production. And nothing is taken away from anybody else; everybody else has exactly the same resources at their disposal that they had prior to my act of production. One person is better off; no one is made worse off.

And finally, acts of voluntary contractual exchange are also productive, in the sense that two individuals expect to benefit from the exchange; otherwise, this voluntary exchange would not have taken place, and again, no resources at the disposal of any third party are affected by this voluntary transaction between two individuals. So, in this case, we have two individuals gaining in utility and satisfaction and nobody losing in utility or satisfaction. Because of this, these three types of activities can be referred to as productive activities, as activities that increase social well-being.

In contrast, we have, of course, what we call parasitic activities and I mean parasitic, this time, in a slightly different meaning from that which I mentioned very early on as having been used by Carroll Quigley. Remember, Quigley refers to parasitic activities as activities that somehow diminish the amount of goods in existence, like picking berries and not replacing them with anything. I would refer to this, under the current definition, as a productive activity, so he uses that term in a slightly different way. At that time when I talked about it, the use of parasitic simply had a different explanatory purpose than the one that I'm using now. What I mean by parasitic in this context is: activities that make some people better off, at the expense of making other people worse off. And those activities would be, obviously, activities such as taking away what some other person has originally appropriated, taking away what some other person has produced, or not waiting for the agreement of some potential exchange partner, but simply robbing him of whatever is his. In this case, in all of these cases, we obviously have a situation where one person gains and another person loses.

Let me briefly mention three typical parasitic activities that play a great role in history, before I then come to a special form of parasitic behavior which is associated with the institution of the state. Parasitic behavior would be, for instance, in the most drastic form, cannibalism. That is, people simply eating another person up. It was, again, insight and intelligence on the part of people that led to the abolition of cannibalism. People realized that yes, in the short run, cannibalism might be beneficial, but if you have a slightly longer-term perspective, you would prefer slavery over cannibalism. This is, indeed, a stage of human development for which we have anthropological evidence. Most cannibals realized, at some point, after smartening up a little bit, that slavery was definitely superior over this, unless you are very, very hungry at this particular moment.

But eventually people even overcame this temptation, and developed slavery. And again, it was rational thought that also overcame this institution of slavery, because they realized that slavery is by and large an unproductive system of human interaction. Again, slavery, in the short run, can, of course, be beneficial if I can use you as my slave for a while, even if I were to recognize that in the long run, I would be better off if you were a free man and I were a free man and we cooperated with each other. In the short run, of course, slavery can have certain advantages and again, it requires a certain development of intelligence, a certain lowering of our time preference, to be willing to give up this immediate advantage that the institution of slavery might represent.

Apart from slavery, of course, the most common form of parasitic behavior is plain crime: robbery and fraud and activities such as those.

And again, we can say that the fact that most people abstain from these types of activities is based on insight, is based on the fact that they realize that in the long run, these things simply do not pay. If robbery were to become common we would all be in terrible shape, but we abstain even from engaging in robbery and fraud, even if we know that, in the short run, we might be able to get away with it. Again, insight, a certain amount of intelligence, a certain ability to delay gratification is necessary on the part of man in order to give up the temptations that these forms of parasitic behavior might represent.

And because of this, because of a certain amount of intelligence, we have reached a stage where cannibalism has basically disappeared, where slavery has basically disappeared, and where fraud and robbery have become rare events, conducted by just a few asocial individuals, and most people abstain from it. So, civilization is maintained by rational insight, by having developed a certain state of intelligence and having lowered our time preference to a certain degree. And again, let me give you a quote to this effect by Mises, and then I will really come to the problem of the origin of the state as I promised. Mises says here,

> One may admit that in primitive man, the propensity for killing and destroying and the disposition for cruelty were innate. We may also assume that under the conditions of earlier ages the inclination to aggression and murder was favorable to the preservation of life. Man was once a brutal beast....But one must not forget that he was physically a weak animal; he would not have been a match for the big beasts of prey, if he had not been equipped with a peculiar weapon, reason. The fact that man is a reasonable being, that he therefore does not yield without inhibitions to every impulse, but arranges his conduct according to reasonable deliberation, must not be called unnatural, from a zoological point of view. Rational conduct means that man, in face of the fact that he cannot satisfy all his impulses, desires and appetites, forgoes the satisfaction of those which he considers less urgent. In order not to endanger the working of social cooperation man is forced to abstain from satisfying those desires whose satisfaction would

> hinder establishment of societal institutions. There is no doubt that such renunciation is painful. However, man has made his choice. He has renounced the satisfaction of some desires incompatible with social life and has given priority to the satisfaction of those desires which can be realized only, or in a more plentiful way, under a system of the division of labor....
>
> This decision is not irrevocable and final. The choice of the fathers does not impair the sons' freedom to choose. They can reverse the resolution. Every day they can proceed to the transvaluation of values and prefer barbarism to civilization, or as some authors say, the soul to the intellect, myth to reason, and violence to peace. But they must choose. It is impossible to have things incompatible with one another.[3]

Now, this fact that mankind has, by and large, developed sufficient reason to engage in cooperation and build a society, has also led, on the other hand, to the temptation of creating a system of institutionalized exploitation or institutionalized parasitism or, as some people have referred to it, stationary banditry. That is, only insofar as we have a rich society before us does the temptation arise for some people to take advantage of the wealth that society has accumulated, to institute a system where they can systematically benefit themselves at the expense of the great masses of productive individuals.

And this brings me to the institution of the state. Let me begin by giving you a definition of what the state is, a definition that is more or less uncontroversial, that you find adopted by practically everyone who talks about this institution. And this definition of the state is that a state is defined as an organization or an agency that exercises a territorial monopoly of ultimate jurisdiction or of ultimate judgeship or of ultimate arbitration in cases of conflict. In particular, it is an institution that is also the ultimate judge, in cases of conflicts involving itself with other people in society. And as a second element of the definition, which is, in a way, already implied in the first one, the state is an

[3]Mises, *Human Action*, pp. 171–72.

organization that exercises a territorial monopoly of taxation. That is, it can determine unilaterally without the consent of others how much the inhabitants of the territory have to pay to the agency of the state for having the state provide this service of being the ultimate judge and arbitrator in the territory.

Now, you immediately recognize from this definition that it is not difficult to explain why people might be motivated to create an institution such as a state. Just imagine what that means. It means that whenever you have conflicts with each other, you must come to me and I settle the conflict and then I tell you what you owe me for the settlement, without receiving or having your consent doing this. This is, of course, a magnificent position to be in. And the position is even better once you recognize that even if I caused a conflict, if I hit someone on the head, then he must come to me and I decide what is right and what is wrong and then, typically I will decide, of course, that what I did was right and what he is doing, complaining about the fact that I hit him on the head, is wrong—and then I tell him in addition that this is the amount of money that you have to pay me for providing you with this magnificent service. It should be very clear from the outset that to explain why there have been attempts to form an institution such as a state is anything but difficult. It is easy as pie to explain why there are constant attempts to try to form institutions such as this, because what more wonderful position could one have, as somebody who has parasitic inclinations, than being in charge of an apparatus such as the state? To explain why there are attempts to found states is a very, very easy thing to do. What is the difficult thing to do is to explain why anybody can get away with this—why people do not prevent such institutions from coming into existence.

And I will turn now to the task, to explain why people would ever have put up with an institution such as this. This explanation becomes even more difficult once you recognize the following, which I call the fundamental law of parasitism. The fundamental law of parasitism is simply this. One parasite can live off a hundred or a thousand hosts very comfortably, but we cannot imagine that thousands of parasites can live a comfortable life off one or two or three hosts. In that case, their life would be miserable too, so what we recognize from this fundamental law of parasitism is that those people who aspire to create an institution such as a state must also always have an interest to be, themselves, just a small group that is capable of ruling, of exploiting, of taxing and exercising an arbitration monopoly over a group of people far larger than they themselves are. And if this is the case, that the state must always attempt to be a very small group as compared to the group which they exploit, then we realize another fundamental insight. Obviously, a small group, very small group, cannot subjugate a large group only by means of brutal force and weapons. Yes, for a short time it might be possible. We can imagine that there are ten people who are all heavily armed. They might control two hundred, three hundred, four hundred people and keep them in subjection, if the people have no arms and the rulers do have arms. But, in the long run, this is very difficult to maintain. That is, we must expect that these four hundred to five hundred people will also find a way to arm themselves—and in that case, how can ten people equipped with arms rule over four hundred to five hundred or thousands of people also equipped with arms and the means to defend themselves? Then, the explanation based on violence, on sheer brute force, this explanation does not work.

What we recognize instead is that the class of parasites, the small group of parasites, must, if it wants to rule over a population for a lengthy period of time, must base its power on popular opinion. That is, it must have at least tacit support among the public. The public must have taken on a position where they put up with this, somehow see a reason for having this institution. The public must have accepted certain ideologies. And this insight, which was first formulated by Étienne de La Boétie and David Hume—and we also find it in Ludwig von Mises and Murray Rothbard—is that the rule of the state over its population depends not on the exercise of sheer brute force, even though that plays some role, but rests fundamentally on nothing other than opinion and tacit agreement on the part of the public.

So then the task becomes to explain the transition from a natural order, as I described it yesterday, from a system of feudalism under which essentially no state organizations existed, to a state of affairs where a stable state institution has come into existence. And let's assume, for a moment, the most favorable situation for state formation without having a state already there. What I mean by this is the following scenario. Let's assume we have a feudal king who is the natural monopolist for conflict resolution. By natural monopolist, I mean every person whenever they have conflicts with each other, do, in fact, go to the king and say, "Come on, you are the most prestigious, most wise and most experienced person. I'll ask you to settle the dispute that I have with this other person." People are entirely free to choose different arbitrators, different judges, but as a matter of fact, they all go to the king to do this. Such a scenario would still be what I call a natural order. The king, in this situation, would receive nothing but rental payments from his own tenants and from the nobles, who would receive rental payments from their own tenants. There's no exploitation of any kind going on. The king does not tax anyone who has property that is independent of the property of the king. The king also does not pass any laws; that is, he does not legislate. Of course, he lays down the rules that his tenants have to follow, but that would be no more than if I'm the owner of a house, then, of course, I lay down certain rules that the tenants of my house have to follow, such as that they have to clean the stairs once a week and things like this. So, this king is part of a natural order and not yet a state king. He neither taxes nor legislates; he only collects rent and lays down the rules of the house of which he himself is the genuine owner.

The decisive step that he must take in order to transform his position into the position of a state would be the following: the king, at one point, would have to say, "From now on, you must come to me whenever you have a conflict with somebody else. You can no longer go to anybody else for conflict resolution. Up to this point, you chose me voluntarily, to be the judge in all cases of conflict. Now, I take away this possibility from you, to turn to others, and I take the right away from others to act, if they should be chosen as judge to do so."

Now, you immediately recognize that by taking this seemingly small step, the king does engage in an act of expropriation. In particular, this act of expropriation is very visible to the other leaders in society, the other nobles, to whom conflicting parties could have turned to receive justice. Again, recall that in the feudal order it was precisely the case that there existed a large number of independent, separate jurisdictions. Each lord was responsible for creating justice within his own territory, over his own property. Now he can no longer do this, so it is in particular the other nobles of whom we would expect to put up resistance against this attempt of the king to monopolize, to acquire the exclusive monopoly. It is no longer a natural monopoly, but it becomes in this case a compulsory monopoly on being the ultimate and final judge in cases of conflict.

How can the king get away with this? The first step—and again, I offer you here not a precise historical description of what happened here or there, but something that you might call a logical reconstruction of what has happened more or less all over the place. The first step is for the king to cause and bring about a crisis situation. And how does he bring about a crisis situation? In a way, that is not very difficult to explain. Just as we recognize how natural, how easy it is to have the motivation to become a state, we can also recognize that among mankind, there exists always the temptation, the itching, especially among the tenants, to free themselves from their rent payments and the rules laid down for them by their own landlords. That is, tenants, wherever you go, you can imagine that it would be not all that difficult to persuade them to engage in some sort of riots against their own landlords. I free you of the rent payment that you must pay. I free you of the disciplinary rules that your landlord imposes on you and I promise to make you a free man. I promise you that you will become the owner of those things which you previously only occupied as a tenant.

Or, in a slightly different scenario, you, as the king, incite a riot among the poor against the rich. You form a coalition with the poor against your own immediate competitors, that is, the well-to-do people in society that somehow are the most direct rivals to the king. So then you create a civil war, that is to say, you create a situation that is similar to the situation that Hobbes claims exists naturally among mankind. Recall, I explained that the natural condition of mankind is not war of all against all. People do recognize that the division of labor is beneficial, and because of this they tend to be in favor of peaceful cooperation, at least the large majority of people do this. But you can incite, especially if you are yourself an influential person, a person who is trusted by the masses, if you are the king, you can incite a situation that brings about a situation such as a war of all against all.

And then, in this situation where the war of all against all breaks out, where the tenants rise against their landlords and the poor rise against the rich, then you come to the rescue of the nobles and the middle classes and strike some sort of compromise. That is, you get a promise from the nobles and your immediate competitors. Yes, we will give up our former right to act as judge ourselves and grant you an exclusive right to be the monopoly judge, in exchange for you and us getting together and stopping this civil war.

This was, by the way, precisely the situation, for instance, during the Middle Ages, especially during the so-called Protestant Revolution, or Protestant Reformation, when first, the Protestant Revolution resulted in big-time looting activities and so forth, and then people turned to the king saying, "This sort of stuff has to be stopped and in order to stop it, we will grant you the exclusive right to be the judge."

So, you create a Hobbesian situation. The Hobbesian situation does not exist from the outset, but it can be created. Again, let me just read you a quote here from Henri Pirenne, who in a slightly different way describes the same phenomenon, that is to say, the king allying himself with the lower classes, with the subnoble classes, so to speak, in order to break the power of the competing aristocracy, of those people who would lose the most from the fact that the king acquires a monopoly. Pirenne there says,

> The clear interest of the monarchy was to support the adversaries of high feudalism. [That is, the adversaries of the noble class, of the aristocracy.] Naturally, help was given whenever it was possible to do so without becoming obligated to [In this case he talks about the cities, the king in particular—he also is inciting the inhabitants of cities to rise against the nobility.] these [city] middle classes who in arising against their lords fought, to all intents and purposes, in the interests of royal prerogatives. To accept the king as arbitrator of their quarrel was, for the parties in conflict, to recognize his sovereignty. The entry of the burghers upon the political scene had as a consequence the weakening of the contractual principle of the Feudal State to the advantage of the principle of the authority of the Monarchical State. It was impossible that royalty

> should not take count of this and seize every chance to show its good-will to the communes which, without intending to do so, labored so usefully in its behalf.[4]

But this is of course only the first step. You create the crisis. The noble class comes to you and wants to be rescued, and you rescue them in exchange for them granting you exclusive judgeship rights. You have to offer something in addition, of course, to the aristocracy. What is typically offered is that the aristocracy now plays some particularly important role in the slowly developing royal bureaucracy that will be established. But more than this, you now need an ideology. Again, recall, without ideological support for it, this institution is not going to last for very long. And the ideology that is created and that is still with us to this day, is the so-called Hobbesian myth. That is, the idea that the normal state of mankind is precisely this war of all against all, which the king deliberately brought about, and that in order to stop this war of all against all, it is necessary that there must be one single monopolist ruling over all people in order to create peace. Now, if you ask yourself—or if you ask all around—ask them why do we need a state? Almost everyone will give you exactly this reason. Without a single monopolist, there would be permanent war of all against all. This is the belief that up to this day has maintained the state apparatus. This is by now a firmly held belief: I have asked my own students and that was the answer that everyone gave. Without the state there would be chaos! There would be no cooperation. There must be a single monopolist. This is the ideology that keeps the state in place.

Let me only point out the following at this point. You can quickly realize the weakness of this ideology, if you do two things. On the one hand, imagine what this means if you have very small groups of people, just two individuals. So, what this theory essentially says is, no two people can ever peacefully cooperate with each other; this would always lead to war of one against the other. There must be always a master and there must be always someone who is subject to the master. You realize immediately, if you just use a very small group of people, how absurd

[4]Henri Pirenne, *Medieval Cities: Their Origins and the Revival of Trade* (1925; Princeton, NJ: Princeton University Press, 1974), pp. 179–80.

this thesis becomes. We have five people. Is it necessary for the group of five people that there must be one person who is the monopolist in every possible conflict, including conflicts involving himself with the other four? For these small groups, most people would immediately say, "You must be crazy to believe this sort of stuff. That can never be true. Because you know groups of this size who peacefully cooperate all the time." Nonetheless, this is one of the implications.

What you recognize here is that they never talk about the size of the territory. And on the other hand, you recognize that if this theory is true, then it must be the case that we must have a world state in order to create peace because the same argument applies, of course, to a situation where we have a multitude of states. If we have a multitude of states, then these various states are in a state of anarchy, of natural order, vis-à-vis each other and allegedly there must be permanent war among them. Now, this is also obviously not the case. There are wars among them, and I will explain why there are more wars among states than there are wars among individuals in one of my next lectures, but it is certainly not the case that states are permanently at war with each other.

What remains entirely unexplained here, and what is somehow taken intuitively for granted, is that we are talking about sizes of states where it is not perfectly clear immediately that these people would peacefully cooperate with each other, but the size of states are, in a way, arbitrary. Why should not a state have the size of a small village for example? In a small village, we have not the slightest difficulty imagining that there can be peaceful cooperation going on without a monopolist. Only when the size becomes a little bit bigger do we become increasingly blind to recognizing that at all times, the same principle is at work, just as the same principle was at work to explain why all of mankind can engage in peaceful cooperation based on the division of labor, why there is not only a reason for the division of labor among the Germans, but the Germans and the French must not fight against each other, why the same principle applies to Germans and to the French. So we have to recognize that this statist principle, if it should be correct, should also apply to the level of you and me. That is to say, I am your slave or you must be my slave, but it is impossible for peaceful cooperation between the two of us to exist.

And once you recognize that the same principle applies, not just to two people, but to the entire world, you recognize immediately that what we have is just a made-up myth, created by this initial crisis that the states themselves or the would-be states created in order to blind people to something that should be perfectly obvious. So now, once a state has established this sort of mythology, they all go through a sequence of steps, essentially the same sequence of steps wherever you look. The first one is, of course, that you have to disarm the population. There existed initially in the Middle Ages independent army leaders offering their army services to whoever needed them: mercenary troops. They are now incorporated into the national army or into the king's army or they are eliminated. Again, all states try to disarm the population.

In the Middle Ages, one of the immediate things that kings did, as soon as they had acquired a semi-state position, was to insist that all the nobles had to raze their own fortresses, to prevent them from coming up with the idea that maybe that whole thing was a screwy process after all and they would defend themselves against the jurisdiction or the tax impositions coming from the side of the king. So, raze your fortresses. You can build nice palaces, but no longer anything that serves defensive purposes.

Then, of course, all independent jurisdictions must be eliminated, ultimately, even going as far as to no longer allowing husbands and wives to be judges in their own homes. This process takes hundreds of years. My reconstruction compresses this into a very short period of time, but all of these powers are gradually won step by step from civil society, and we have basically only now, in the twentieth century, reached the point where the power of the state extends as far as involving itself in immediate family affairs, like daring, for instance, to take children away from their parents. This is something that would not have been possible hundreds of years ago; the power of the kings was not sufficient from the outset to do something like this, but we realize that now the power of the state is large enough to tell you whether you can smoke in your own house or not.

The next step is very important: to control the ideology, to keep alive this belief in the Hobbesian myth and the necessity of the state for the creation of peace. And for this you have to take over, you will first try to take over, the churches. This occurs with the Protestant Revolution, as a result of which a far closer alliance between church and state is built than existed prior to this. By the way, that's why the Protestant Revolution was supported by so many princes, because they realized that that was exactly offering them the opportunity to establish themselves as states, besides the obvious motive that they could also grab property from the Catholic Church, which, in some countries, made up 20–30 percent of the used landmass. And, it offered them a great opportunity to just enrich themselves greatly by expropriating the churches.

And then, of course, you introduce successively public education, by controlling the church, given that the church was a main instructional institution for a long period of time, and making the priests state employees. This has, of course, happened in all European countries, to a larger or smaller extent, particularly in the Protestant countries where all priests are paid according to the official pay scale that regulates how other bureaucrats are paid. And if this does not go far enough, then, of course, you create a system of public education under direct state control. Martin Luther, for instance, played a great role in this, advising the princes not only to oppress the peasants (whom he had first brought to rise against the princes, but then smashed them down), but also advised the princes that just as the people should be trained in order to be ready for war, so they should also be brainwashed in state-controlled schools in order to become brave and well-trained citizens.

And the last step, after the nationalization of education, is the control of money, that is, the monopolization of the issuance of money. There existed, for instance, in France, before the establishment of a central French king, a multitude of mints competing against each other, trying to acquire the reputation of producing the best, most reliable, least manipulated, type of money. All these competing mints were gradually closed down, until, in the end, only one central government mint remained in existence, which, of course, makes it far easier to engage in manipulations of the gold or silver content than it would be if there were a multitude of mints competing against each other. If you have a multitude of mints competing against each other, each mint has an incentive to point out if another one is defrauding you. You have a mint from town A or town B, they are engaging in coin clipping so people would respond by bankrupting or boycotting this type of mint. As soon as only one mint exists to serve a large territory, it becomes far easier to engage in these sorts of manipulations and thereby having a tool for enriching yourself, in addition to your power to tax.

Lastly, they also then monopolize the means of transportation and communication, which is of great importance once you recognize that means of communication and transportation would have to play a very important role in any attempt to revolt against the government. You have to move troops from place to place; you have to send letters and messages from place to place, so you monopolize the postal service and you monopolize at least the main throughways and make them the king's roads and the king's postal service, in order to control the public.

I will end with a few additional observations. With states coming into existence, the normal natural tendencies for markets to expand, division of labor to expand and intensify, is not brought to a halt, but it is somehow distorted and disrupted. There exist now, all of a sudden, state borders that previously did not exist, and automatically, once you have state borders, the possibility arises that you can now hamper and interfere with the free flow of goods. That is, you can impose tariffs. Second, the normal tendency of money to become an international money is also brought to a halt because now we have borders. There will be national monies arising, even if they are initially commodity monies, but they will now be French francs and Italian lira, and this brings about monetary disintegration, or reduces the amount of integration that would otherwise naturally arise on the market. Then, with the existence of the state, of course, the tendency for law to become universal and international, that I described in my lecture yesterday, is slowed down or halted. We had these insurance agencies and reinsurance agencies and arbitration agencies and the conflict between various insurance agencies leading, then, to the competitive development of universally accepted standards of right and wrong, of what is legal and illegal; this comes to a halt. Law is now broken up into German law, Dutch law, Swedish law, every country having different sorts of principles, procedures, etc. The tendency that normally exists for unifying this comes to a halt.

And last but not least, states also have a profound effect on the development of languages. On the one hand, they sometimes forcibly expand certain types of languages within their territory, eliminate certain languages and make some languages the official language of the country. On the other hand, by doing this, as the other side of the same coin, they also disrupt the natural tendency of people to learn different languages and on the fringes of different territories for people to speak multiple languages and, in a way, also prevent the development of some languages that are used as international languages. Just think of what happened to Latin, which used to be the language of international communication for hundreds of years all throughout Europe. Latin basically disappears from this function as soon as national states come into existence. It is then that French is spoken, German is spoken and Latin becomes, if it does not die out immediately, a language that is spoken less and less and in the end, it becomes just a relic that some strange people still learn in strange places without really knowing why, because nobody except the pope and his people actually speak that language.

LECTURE 8

From Monarchy to Democracy

THE SUBJECT OF THIS LECTURE is "From Monarchy to Democracy." This is obviously one of the main subjects that I cover in my book *Democracy: The God That Failed*. I have talked about monarchs already in the previous two lectures, about the role of monarchs in feudal societies, which we can refer to as prestate societies. And then, in the last lecture, about the position of monarchs as heads of state and the transition from the feudal stage to the monarchical state. Roughly speaking, historically, and only talking about Europe, in this case the period of feudal monarchs is roughly the period from 1100 to 1500 and then from 1500 until the end of World War I, that is, the period of monarchical states. The later stages are constitutional monarchical states and the earlier stages are what we refer to typically as absolute monarchies. As I said, the discussion during the last two lectures referred mostly to the development in Europe. I will come back to the European development, that is, to Christian monarchies as a transition from Christian monarchs to democracy in a moment, but I want to say a few things about the institution of kings and monarchs in general, even outside of the European scenery.

In a way, monarchs are a more typical form of rulership, whether pre-state or state rulers, than any other form. Democracies are a very rare event in human history, and it is easy to explain why that is, because patriarchy is one of the most natural institutions that you can imagine. You have, of course, fathers as the heads of households, and by and large the idea of kings was modeled after the structure that you find in households. Kings were typically regarded as the heads of extended families or the heads of clans or the heads of tribes, or later on of course, the heads of entire nations, but developing along the lines of the idea that this is a natural development, similar to what we see in each family.

All kings try to associate themselves with some sort of religious, or give themselves some sort of religious, dignity. In many places on the globe, kings were considered to be either gods or incarnations of gods or descendants of gods or as people who acquired godlike status after their deaths. And kings in all societies tried in a way to provide two functions. On the one hand, the function as judge and priest, that is, as the intellectual head of larger groups of people, and on the other hand, the function as warrior and protector of their clans or tribes or whatever the group was of which they were considered to be the head. And while it was sometimes the case that these two functions, the priest-judge function and the warrior-protector function were separated and occupied by different individuals, there was always an attempt made to combine the two, to make the protector and warrior also, at the same time, the high priest, and of course, in combining these two functions, you would achieve a far greater power than if these two functions were somehow exercised by different individuals controlling each other.

Outside of the West, more typically it was the case that the king was also considered to be the head of the religious organization or the head of the church. That was the case in places like Egypt and also in Japan, in the Islamic world, with the Hindus, and also in the case of China; the uniqueness of Western civilization, as I mentioned in the previous lectures, was precisely the relatively strict separation of these two functions by different individuals and different institutions. This is not to say that this existed all throughout the West, and it certainly was the case that religious leaders might hope and try to acquire earthly powers and that the earthly rulers try to control the churches. But certainly from about the year 1000 or so, this separation between the two roles worked for quite some time in Europe, basically until the Protestant Revolution when the combination between church, on the one hand, and state or earthly rulers, on the other hand, became increasingly closer again.

This separation between church leaders and the earthly worldly rulers did not, of course, prevent the various kings from claiming some sort of elevated status for themselves. I mentioned in the previous lecture that the kings of England, for instance, tried to trace their own claims to the land back to Adam and Eve, and thereby present themselves as people whose position had ultimately been founded by God, and that all of their subjects were indeed nothing else but the offspring following the tenants of Adam and Eve. Nonetheless, at least for the Christian world, even if kings claim that they have this special historical dignity of having been installed by God directly or indirectly into their positions, precisely because in Christianity kings are not considered to be godlike figures and we have a transcendent God, kings were always considered to be under the law like everyone else. And because of this, in the West, the institution of regicide, killing the king, was always considered to be quite legitimate, not entirely undisputed, but for centuries, of course, considered to be something that was entirely alright, if the king would not do what he was supposed to do, according to the universal law laid down by the transcendent God.

In addition, in Europe, or at least in some parts of Europe, the power of the king was always restricted by the fact that there existed other noblemen who claimed to be the sole and exclusive owners of their land, that is, not to have received their land as some sort of grant from the king, but being, maybe on a smaller scale, but nonetheless, an equally safe private property owner as a king was of whatever he claimed to be his. This is what we refer to as the *allodial* form of feudalism. And given, at least for the feudal king, that he was recognized as a voluntarily acknowledged judge and military leader, as I explained in the previous lecture, it took quite some time for him to secure and gain the position as a sovereign, stripping these allodial feudal owners of their full and complete property rights and establishing himself as a compulsory monopolist.

Now, with the establishment of kings as heads of states, we can almost from the very beginning discover the seeds of the destruction of dynastic monarchies in the following way. Remember what I explained about the justification that was given for the existence of a state, the justification that Hobbes developed. There will be war of all against all, and the only way that we can create peace is by having one monopolist on top of the social hierarchy being the ultimate judge equipped with the power to tax. Now, interestingly, in this justification, you realize that it doesn't really matter for the Hobbesian argument who this monopolist is. It happened to be monarchs at the time because the institution of monarchy is a relatively natural institution, just people who have more wisdom and riches accumulated and who command more authority and are looked up to.

The first governments, the first states, happen to be monarchical states, but the argument for the state that monarchs used, in order to establish themselves as a state, makes no reference to a claim that it must be a king who is this monopolist. In principle, it can be anyone, it just must be a monopolist who does it. Because of this, for instance, the English kings were initially quite unsympathetic toward the Hobbesian argument, because they realized that it did not contain a specific justification or legitimation for the institution of dynastic monarchs, and Hobbes was even suspected of having some sort of republican sympathies, or even as being somebody who might have secret sympathies for Cromwell. Whether that is true or not is irrelevant, but what is of importance is the fact that this justification for the state, this rational justification for the state, embodies the seeds of the destruction of the institution of a monarchical state.

Now, this transition from monarchical state to a different form of state democracy took several hundred years, just as the establishment of states out of prestate orders took several hundred years, and the transition was driven not least by the very intellectuals that played an important role in securing the position of kings as states. Remember, states need legitimacy, need support, voluntary support among the public, and it was precisely intellectuals that were hired by the king who spread this idea about the necessity of a monopolist judge equipped with taxing power. But as intellectuals happen to be, they are always unsatisfied with their own position, even though the position of theirs somehow improved, being now somewhat employed or semi-employed by kings. As soon as they had reached this position, they began to spread various egalitarian views, and these egalitarian views simply raised the question whether it isn't somehow unjust that there exist people who have privileges, that the king is guided by a different type of law than the rest of mankind, that there are princely laws and privileges different from the laws and rules that apply to the rest of mankind. So, the egalitarian propaganda took the form of an attack against privilege. How can privilege be squared with the Christian idea that we are all created equal by the same creator—and the alleged solution proposed to this seeming injustice was to say that there should be open entry into the position of government. Why should it be the king? After all, only a state was necessary in order to create law and order, and other people could do that just as well as some sort of hereditary king could do it. There were some people early on who recognized that the problem was rather that the state king represented a monopoly, and that what was necessary as a solution was, in a way, to get rid of this monopoly power—again, to have competing jurisdictions. But the overwhelming majority took the line that in order to abolish privileges, all we have to do is open up entry into the government to everyone, and they called this equality before the law.

Now, I point out from the outset that there is, of course, an error involved in this. By opening entry into the government agency to everyone instead of restricting it to just the members of some specific family, you do not abolish privileges. What you achieve instead is that you now substitute functional privileges for personal privileges. The king and his successors had a personal privilege, but if you open entry to the position of the government leader to everyone, you still have a functional privilege. Everyone can now acquire this privileged position, but there still exists privileged positions. In legal terms, you can say, instead of having a higher princely law and a lower law applying to the common man, we have now created, so to speak, public law, that is, the law that regulates the behavior of those who are in charge of the state, and private law that applies to the rest of mankind.

But, public law is, again, superior over private law in the same way as princely law was superior over the law applying to common folks. Public law beats private law, and that there are privileges you can simply see by the fact that as a public official, you could do things that you were not allowed to do as a private individual. This is, of course, true up to this day. As a public official, you can take the property of others. As a private citizen, this would be considered to be a crime.

As a public official, you can enslave people; you can draft them into the army and military. If you were just a plain private individual, then that same act would be considered to be an outrage and would be a punishable offense. Privileges do not disappear when you open entry to government to everyone, and not everyone is equal before the law either, because there exist two types of law. If you are a public official, a different law applies to you and protects you than if you were a private individual; as a private individual you are only protected by a subordinate form of law, that is private law.

If we look at the change from monarchy to democracy, described as a system where entry into the government is available to everyone, from a purely economic point of view, what happens in this case is that we substitute a person who considers the entire territory over which he exercises monopolistic control as his private property which he can pass on to his offspring, for a person who is only a temporary caretaker who is in charge, for a certain limited period of time, of the same territory. But this, being the owner of a territory versus being a temporary caretaker of a territory, makes a fundamental difference from an economic point of view. Let me just illustrate that by using a very elementary example. I can give you a house and say, "You are the owner of the house. You can sell this house if you want, you can pass it on to future generations if you want. You can sell part of it. You have the right to collect rent from it." And on the other hand, I give you a house and say, "You are not the owner of the house. You cannot sell it, you cannot determine who will be your successor. You can also not sell part of it, but you can use it to your own advantage for a certain period of time. That is, the rent that you can get out of this house, you are free to do with this rental income whatever you want."

Now, ask yourself whether or not these two people will treat the house in the same way or differently, and the answer is obvious. There will be a fundamental difference in the way that the house will be treated by these two individuals. The incentive for the owner is, yes, of course, I try to get as high a rental income as possible out of the house, but at the same time, I always take into consideration what happens to the value of the capital stock of which I am the owner. After all, I can sell the house. Or, I can pass the house on to future generations. And it is possible, for instance, to increase your rental income from your house in such a way that the value of the capital stock drops or falls more than my increase in rental income that I get. An owner would try to prevent something like this from happening. And if he doesn't do this, then he will be punished insofar as he will see that the value of his property will fall in the property market. A caretaker's incentives are entirely different. A caretaker only owns the rental income. He does not own the capital stock. What is his incentive? His incentive is to maximize his rental income regardless of what the repercussions are with respect to the value of the capital stock.

Let's say that instead of putting one or two families in my house and collecting rent from two families, I can instead put a thousand guest workers in my house and have one bed over the other and thereby I will definitely increase my rental income. But it is also easy to see what the price of this type of usage will be, that is, there will be a deterioration of the property taking place very quickly. The toilets will be clogged immediately, the carpets will be dirtied. There will be graffiti on the walls and all the rest of it, people come home drunk and smash the walls and who knows what. Again, if I know that I will be in charge of this house for four years and that the losses in terms of the capital value are not my losses because I don't own the thing in the first place, my incentive will be to maximize my current income that can be achieved by using this capital, even if it is the case that at the end of these four years, the capital stock has been run into the ground and has been completely depleted.

Now, on a large scale, this is the difference between democratic caretakers of countries and kings as owners of countries. A democratic caretaker's incentive is that I have to loot the country as fast as possible, because if I don't loot it as fast as possible, then I will no longer be in power. I can buy myself many, many friends if I just impose a tremendous amount of taxes right now, and as to what happens after I am out of power, who cares? Whereas kings, at least by and large, had an interest in preserving the value of their dynastic property and passing on a valuable piece of property to future generations. No, I'm not saying that every king will automatically be equally good in terms of preserving his capital values, nor do I say that every single democratic caretaker will precisely follow the scenario that I developed, but what I'm saying is, the incentive structure is so different that we can expect that by and large, on the average, kings will have a longer planning horizon and a greater interest in the preservation of the capital stock and democratic rulers, by and large, have a far smaller interest in the preservation of the capital stock and a far greater interest in the current consumption of resources that you can press out of the existing capital stock. The exploitation of a king is a long-run exploitation, farsighted exploitation, calculated exploitation. The exploitation of a democratic caretaker is short-run exploitation, noncalculating exploitation, and so on.

I will illustrate this by looking just at three dimensions here. The subject of taxation—for a king, of course, he wants to tax, there's no question. Everybody is tempted to do this; if you have the right to tax, of course you like to tax. But, what he will bring into perspective is, if I tax too much right now, the productivity of the population might go down in the long run and I expect to be in power also in the long run. So, he will more likely engage in a moderate amount of taxation, always keeping in mind the disincentive to productive people that taxation implies. Compare this with a caretaker who is just in charge for a certain period of time. Again, for him, the fact that in the long run, productivity will decline if he currently engages in massive amounts of taxation is of far lesser concern than it would be for a king because after all, in the more distant future, he will likely not be in power. He is far more present oriented in this regard, and discounts the fact that high taxation means a reduction in productivity on the part of the subject population to a greater extent than a king would do.

Look at the subject of debt, of state debt. A king is, of course, also inclined to incur debt and they all did, especially for war finance, but kings typically, in order to get credit, had to pledge certain things as security and in addition, though that was somewhat disputed, there was always the possibility that the future generations were held responsible for the debt incurred by their own father or mother. That was not in all cases carried through, but it was hanging as a Damoclean sword above the head of a king that maybe the next generation is expected to pay off my debt. And again, he knows, of course, that if his debt load is too high, this has long-run negative repercussions on savings rates, and he tries to avoid these long-run consequences, to a certain extent at least. Now consider a public caretaker and his attitude toward government debt. First of all, none of these people ever expects that any of them will be held personally responsible for the debt to be repaid. Ronald Reagan, who indebted the United States more than anybody before him and now, our beloved Bush warrior, who again, indebts this country for a tremendous amount—Reagan is not in debtor's prison, nor will Bush have to fear that he will be jailed if he doesn't repay the debt. They just take up as much debt as they can, and say that some future suckers will have to pay for this. In addition, of course, they will not give any security for it. That is, whereas major lenders to kings insisted that if you don't repay, I get this castle or that castle or this little piece of land or that piece of land from you. Here there are no pledges of any security whatsoever. If a democratic government defaults on their debt, none of you are entitled to take over the Grand Canyon or some place like this, so no security whatsoever. And again, you can, of course, imagine that the tendency of democratic governments to run up debts is far more pronounced than it would be under monarchical rule.

The same applies to inflation. Yes, of course, kings loved inflation, coin clipping and so forth; it enriches you. But again, there are two concerns that you have. On the one hand, by inflating, you increase your own current income; on the other hand, you will get, in the future, taxes back in inflated money. For people who have a very short-term perspective, what counts far more is the current advantage that you have in terms of inflating, that you can print the money and then buy yourself a Mercedes or a BMW or whatever you want. And then you realize, of course, how many friends you have that you were not even aware of, who also just realized that man, these guys have the magic wand, they can just create wealth merely by printing up paper money. Yes, of course, you get inflated paper money in the form of future taxes back too, but again, in the future, you will not be there; you will not be the recipient of that inflated money that comes back in the form of taxes. Then, your attitude toward inflation is more generous, so to speak. You like inflation more.

Again, for all of these predictions that I make, there exists, of course, ample empirical evidence that this is indeed the case. Let me just emphasize that while kings tried several times to substitute paper monies for commodity monies such as gold or silver, all of these attempts were relatively short-lived attempts. And they had to go back to a gold or silver standard. For the democratic world, which begins after World War I—during this period, for the first time in all of human history, it happens that commodity monies disappear entirely on a worldwide scale and wherever you go, all you have is paper money, and of course, paper money inflation on a scale that was unheard of in previous centuries.

There's also a different attitude among kings, as compared to democratic caretakers, when it comes to the redistribution of income. Both can take other people's property, but the king, if he takes property from private individuals, runs an ideological danger. That is, he himself vis-à-vis other kings, considers himself also to be a private property owner. He does not want to undermine the legitimacy of private property, because if he does, then, of course, his competitors, King George or King Henry or whatever, King Fritz, they might then be interested in also taking his property. So, he's very much interested in maintaining the legitimacy of the institution of private property as such. So, his forms of redistribution are rarely redistributions from the rich to groups of poor. The redistribution activities through which he tries to achieve popularity are typically benefits that he gives to particular individuals in the form of privileges, and mostly to individuals who have achieved something. Just take the Hapsburgs as an example. They sometimes ennobled people who were enemies of monarchy, but in most cases they ennobled people who had achieved something. That's why the family of Ludwig von Mises was ennobled, despite the fact that they were Jewish. They also had relatively little racial hatreds, because all the noble houses were somehow interconnected and there was sort of far more international orientation among the kings than among democratic caretakers, who tend to be more nationalistic.

The redistribution under democratic conditions is different. You have to be reelected all the time and you have to be reelected by the masses, and the masses always consist of have-nots. There are always more have-nots than haves, in every dimension of having that is worth having. That is, in terms of money, in terms of beauty, in terms of smarts, whatever it is, there always exist more dummies than smarts; there always exists more poor than rich, etc. The strategy under democratic systems is, of course, the redistribution of income. First of all, you don't have to legitimize this anymore because after all, you are now operating no longer as somebody who defends the principle of private property; you are in favor of public property and consider public property to be superior to or more important than private property. Taking private property is no ideological problem for you, and then, of course, you distribute it not to individuals, but to the masses, and by and large, to the masses of have-nots, that is, the less capable people in all dimensions of capability.

Then I come to the argument that is frequently brought up in favor of democracy, that is, "Shouldn't we, as free marketeers, be in favor of free entry? After all, this is what we learned in economics: monopoly is bad, from the point of view of consumers, because there is no longer free entry into every line of production. And if there is no longer free entry into every line of production, then the incentive of a producer to produce at the lowest possible cost is no longer in existence." Imagine this: if there exists free entry in the free market, everybody can become a car manufacturer, for instance. Then, if I produce a car at a cost that is higher than the minimum possible cost of producing this car, I basically extend an invitation to somebody else to go into competition against me, to produce the same product at a lower cost than my cost and then be able, of course, to charge a lower price for the product and thereby drive me out of the market. On the other hand, if we have restrictions on free entry, then this pressure to produce at the lowest possible cost is no longer operative. This is the case that we make, normally, for why we are in favor of competition, meaning free entry into every line of production, and why we are against monopoly, meaning entrance into certain lines of production is either prohibited or obstacles are placed in the way of free entry, etc. The argument of some advocates of democracy goes, "Yeah, isn't the same thing true here? If we have a king, meaning restricted entry, and with democracy, all of a sudden entry is open, and isn't this a big advantage of democracy over monarchy?"

Now, the problem with this argument is this. The argument against monopoly in favor of competition that I presented before only holds insofar as we are considering the production of goods. The argument, however, does not hold if we consider the production of bads, and this is precisely what governments do. After all, people who are taxed do not willingly pay for the privilege of being taxed. That is to say, they are not considering being taxed to be a good. Those people who are, through legislative action, stripped of their property or robbed of part of their income, do not consider that to be a good thing that happens to them; they consider that to be a bad. People who see that the purchasing power of their money goes down as a result of paper money printing, do not consider this the production of goods; they consider that as the production of something bad. Now, do we want to have competition in the areas of the production of bads? The answer should be obvious: no. In the production of bads, we want to have as little competition as there can possibly be. We do not want to have competition as to who would be the most efficient commandant of a gas chamber. We would not want to have competition as to who would be the best whipper of slaves. There, we would be perfectly happy if that slave-whipping or gas chamber-commandant occupation would be very restricted and we would be quite happy if very incompetent people exercise this power, rather than looking for people who are particularly good at this.

Continuing this argument, you might say, "Kings, because they get into their position by accident of birth, can, of course, be evil guys, no question about it." But, if they are evil guys and pose a danger that, through their activity, the possession of their dynasty—after all, they are head of a family—is threatened, then what typically happens is that one of their close relatives will be designated to make short shrift of this guy and chop off his head. That is, we have a way of getting rid of these people, and we don't even have to worry too much about the general public taking care of this problem. It is within the family of those weird kings themselves where they have the greatest incentive either to surround these weirdos with advisors who curtail their evil desires, or if this doesn't work, then have somebody hired out of their own family to kill this guy off.

On the other hand, if you come into the position by accident, it is also possible that these people can be nice and decent people, like nice uncles. They do not have to worry about being reelected. They have been by and large trained for a long time to be the future king or queen and to take care of the country. And believe me, I have met some members of royal houses; the upbringing of those people on the average tends to be an upbringing that most people would not like to suffer. That is to say, there is far more demanded of them in terms of decent good behavior than of the normal run-of-the-mill-type people. I'm glad that I'm not one of the offspring of a royal house. There is, in most of these places, relatively little fun in your life. In those monarchical families that have been deposed, they have frequently become playboys, because they have had no preparation for anything else. They just have affairs and gamble and do this and that, but in those places where there is still the expectation that they will get into the position, I tell you, there is discipline that you have never seen in your own house before.

Now look at democratic rulers and how they get to power. They have to be elected. And, it should be perfectly clear, that under this condition, that is, with free entry, everyone can become president, senator, etc.—and these people are in the business of doing bad things, being capable of doing bad things; we have a competition, "Who is the smartest bad guy? Who has the most demagogic talent? Who is a magnificent briber, liar, cheater and all the rest of it?" Under democratic conditions, especially on the central level, it is almost impossible that a decent person will ever be elected to a higher rank. This might not be the case in a small village. In a small village, there are still some sort of social constraints, as the biggest, smoothest liar and so forth might not win an election in a village of one hundred people where everybody knows what kind of jerk he is. But, go to higher levels, state level, federal level, etc., it is almost assured that a person who out of conviction, doesn't lie, who says we should, of course, not rip off the rich in order to give to the poor, but we should protect private property rights under all circumstances, a person like this is as likely to be elected as that it will snow in the summer in Las Vegas.

I will just make a few more remarks. There is also far more resistance against raising taxes if you have monarchs in place because everybody sees, this is a monarch, I cannot be the monarch. I'm just a regular guy and why should he tax me? There will be resistance against being taxed because you realize you will never benefit from this sort of stuff. On the other hand, as soon as everybody has a chance to become president, senator, or whatever it is, you do not like being taxed as long as you are outside of government, but there is a consolation prize. The consolation prize may be that at one point I will be at the other end of all of this, and that makes me put up with the taxation more easily than I otherwise would. That's another important argument. Again recall, kings that overdo it, they quickly lose their heads. Democrats, even if they are far more evil than kings ever would be, because you think, "Maybe in four years we can get rid of this guy, he will rarely be killed, and imagine how nice it would be if this institution of regicide would also be expanded to democraticide or something of that nature."

I will end on some offside remarks. The first one explains how I developed these ideas about monarchy. The person who made me interested in this subject in the first place was Eric von Kuehnelt-Leddihn, with whom I was somewhat friends. He was, of course, far older than I am. Before that, like most people, I always thought, "Monarchy, what an idiotic thing to say. How can you even talk about this subject?" So, he convinced me that that was something worthwhile thinking about. I think he did not have nearly as convincing arguments as those I later developed. [Laughter] I'm not boasting, because he himself admitted that. He wrote a few articles before he died and in each one, he quotes me and says that I have, of course, developed this far further than he ever thought possible. So, it is not that I just boast about this.

The idea that I stumbled across first, from which I then developed this was, having observed that in the former Soviet Union, in contrast to most places on Earth, in the last two decades, life expectancies fell. Having traveled extensively in the Eastern Bloc because my parents came from East Germany and were exploited by the government there, and I have relatives there and visited these places, I always noticed the bad health conditions of these people, despite the fact that they had, of course, free healthcare. There, everything was free, except nothing was ever available of these allegedly free things. And I asked myself, "What could explain this? If life expectancy falls here but everywhere else it seems to be going up." And another striking observation was the massive number of people that the Soviet Union killed and worked to death, even during peacetime.

And then it came upon me, there's actually a very simple explanation for this and the explanation is simply this. There exist two types of slavery. There exists the old run-of-the-mill-type slavery that we are familiar with in the United States. You Americans are familiar with it and guilty; I, of course, am not. Germans have done other things, but not that. So, here you had private ownership of slaves. In the Soviet Union and in the Eastern Bloc countries, you also had a form of slavery, because slavery is characterized by two marks. On the one hand, you cannot run away. If you try to run away, and they catch you, they punish you or even kill you. And the second characteristic is that they can assign you to work. This they could do in the Soviet Union. You could not run away, they would shoot you dead if you tried to do this and of course you could not just hang around. If you were just hanging around, they would take you and put you to work someplace. But, the slaves in the Soviet Union were not privately owned slaves. That is, Lenin, Stalin, and Gorbachev and whomever, they could not sell these people in the slave market and pocket the money, or rent them out for a few hours and then finance their beers from the rental money that they got. No, they were just public owners or public caretakers of these slaves. They could exploit them to the hilt, but they did not own the capital in them. That is, they did not own the person. And once you realize this, then it is perfectly clear that a private slave owner who can sell the slave in the slave market, who can rent him out, who can pass him on to his son, will by and large treat his slave far more humanely than somebody who is a public slave owner, because the private slave owner realizes that if he mistreats a slave, the value of that slave will fall.

What private slave owner would, just for the joy of it, kill the slave? That is a very rare event. Just like a farmer doesn't kill his horses and cows just for the fun of it. After all, they represent his capital goods! But in the Soviet Union, in those places where you had public slavery, this is precisely what happened. People did not take care of their slaves. Life expectancy fell. If these slaves dropped like flies, no problem, you had a fresh supply waiting just around the corner. If you were told that you must be a slave, that you can't be a free man, what would you choose? Would you want to be a privately owned slave or would you want to be a gulag slave? And I think the answer is perfectly clear. I'd rather be a privately owned slave than a gulag slave. And when it comes to democracy and monarchy, the thing is basically the same. If you cannot be a free man, if you cannot have a natural order that respects private property, but you have to be ripped off by somebody, would you rather want to be ripped off by some dynasty of kings or by some randomly elected caretakers? And I think the answer to this question is also relatively clear.

And the last thing I want to do is, again, give you an example that I always give to my students and, based on their reaction, always find very instructive, explaining the effects of democracy. You know that during the twentieth century, the right to vote was extremely restricted. In many countries, it didn't exist at all early in the nineteenth century, but then it was gradually expanded over time. First, of course, people only thought about male franchise. Females were considered to be just appendices of men, voting just like their husbands do. Unfortunately, they don't do that anymore either.

And the interesting thing is, the country, for instance, that introduced the male franchise first, almost full male franchise, happened to be the country that gave the right to vote to women last, and that was Switzerland. And since that time, Switzerland is also in a very iffy condition. They were already in great danger before, but the danger has dramatically increased since that time. But, as you realize, of course, I have nothing against women at all. I'm a lover of women and I'm just in favor of nobody should have the right to vote. But in any case, in the nineteenth century, gradually the franchise was expanded and parallel to the expansion of the franchise, the classical liberal movement died out and social democratic and socialist parties came to power. Even those parties who called themselves liberal are no longer liberal in the previous classical sense. They have become social liberal parties.

And in order to illustrate this tendency, to make people understand this, as almost a necessary consequence of expanding the franchise, I always use two examples. The first example is, imagine we have a world democracy, one man, one woman, one vote, on a worldwide scale. What will the result of that be? There will be an Indian-Chinese coalition government, simply by virtue of numbers. What will this Indian-Chinese coalition government do, in order to be reelected in the next round? They will, of course, initiate a massive redistribution, an income and wealth redistribution program from the United States and Western Europe to those regions. Does anybody have the slightest doubt that that would be the result? I have not found any student in my classes who ever had the slightest doubt that that is what would happen. And then, you point out, "Look, what do you think happened when they expanded the franchise in your own country?" And then they begin to realize, oh, that's probably exactly the same thing happened there too, maybe not as drastically because the population was more homogeneous, the difference between income levels were not as pronounced as they are now between India and the United States or places like this, but of course, the same thing has happened there.

And the second example is, in the nineteenth century, the age when people could vote was relatively high and by and large, they also had property restrictions. But, look just at the age. There were many places like Italy, where the age was twenty-nine years, in a country with a life expectancy of forty-five. So, only old men could vote in that place. That would be nowadays like only people above seventy-five years would be allowed to vote. And then the voting age was gradually reduced to its current level of eighteen. Now, we have to admit that eighteen is, of course, a completely arbitrary age. Why not twelve? In many places of the world, people can write at age twelve. In the United States, that is not always clear, but many places, it is known of people that they are able to write. So, why not twelve? Now, what would then happen? I would not predict that a twelve-year-old would then be elected president or something like this, but what you can predict is, of course, that every political party would have something on their platform about the legitimate concerns and rights of the children. Just as we are nowadays greatly concerned about the elderly, that we treat them right because we know they have the most time on their hands and tend to go and schlep out to these elections, whereas other people sometimes have to work and can't go. We would then be greatly concerned about their well-being and what would these platforms then likely contain? At least one visit to Toys "R" Us per month, free videos from Blockbuster, as many as you want, at least one square meal at McDonald's, or Burger King per day and a Big Gulp for every kid at all times.

LECTURE 9

State, War, and Imperialism

TODAY I WANT TO TALK about state, war, and imperialism. I want to begin by reminding you that fighting and war, conquest, and plunder are part of human history, despite the advantages of the division of labor, about which I have talked extensively. And if we look for reasons for this deviationist behavior, we will find three factors. One is a lack of intelligence, and closely correlated with that is a very high time preference. High time preference and low intelligence are closely correlated phenomena, being just concerned with immediate effects, not being able to grasp the long-run advantages that result from the division of labor, but being tempted by the immediate advantages that you can gain by robbing and plundering and engaging in these sorts of activities. And the third factor that contributes to it is violent ideologies. There exist ideologies like ardent nationalism and things of that nature that have also mightily contributed to the fact of war. We just have to think of the current Iraq War the idea that some countries are simply superior to others, due to who knows what, obviously contributes to these types of wars.

Nonetheless, I want to emphasize before I get to the subject of war in history, that there has also been a peaceful spread of civilization. Just recall what I talked about very early in my lectures, the slow and gradual outward expansion of agricultural life from the Fertile Crescent, progressing from that area by about one kilometer per year, for several thousand years, gradually displacing the less civilized societies of hunters and gatherers and herders, and instituting more peaceful social relations than existed before. Or, think of examples of colonialism, which is something very different from imperialism. Colonialism was driven by the motive of scarcity of land, and also driven by various missionary ideologies, Christians wanting to spread the Christian belief to other areas.

Just to give you a few examples of relatively peaceful colonial adventures, such as Greek colonialism, without which we would not have had cities like Stagira, where Aristotle was born, or Pestamus, or Pergamon, or Efesus, or Agrigento, or Syracuse, all of which are Greek in origin, and places to which the Greek culture was exported. Similarly, we can say that, at least partially, primitive Rome also had a civilizing effect on the rest of Italy, carrying its superior culture to less developed places in Italy and also to less developed places in parts of the later Roman Empire. Without colonialism by the Bavarians, there would be no such thing as Austria, which was, at that time, on the eastern fringes of civilization, and Bavarians settled these regions and turned them into more or less civilized places. We should mention the efforts of Frederick the Great and Maria Theresia, who promoted the settlement of Germans in more eastern regions of Europe with the purpose of lifting cultural life in those regions. Or, coming to more modern times, New France, Canada: in 1754 there were 55,000 people from France who settled in Canada and created, so to speak, civilization out of nothing. After 1650, some 80,000 people settled in New England and more than 100,000 settled in Maryland and Virginia. All in all, some 2 million people left Britain during the seventeenth and eighteenth centuries for colonial purposes, by and large peaceful ventures. Some 200,000 Germans left for America before 1800.

Let me give you some numbers of countries where people left and countries to which people went, from the mid-nineteenth century to about 1930. All in all, 52 million Europeans left Europe during that period of time. Five million Austrians left their country, 18 million Britons, less than 5 million Germans, 10 million Italians, about 5 million Spaniards, about 2 million Russians and slightly less than 2 million Portuguese. And where did they go? Six million of them went to Argentina, more than 4 million went to Brazil, more than 5 million went to Canada, 34 million went to the United States, slightly less than 3 million went to Australia, about half a million went to New Zealand, and slightly less than half a million went to South Africa. There's also an interesting fact that close to 4 million people went to Siberia during the nineteenth century, that is, into an area that was basically nothing before. And last, but not least, by 1930 or so, some 8 million Chinese had left their country and gone to various Southeast Asian places and lifted up their cultures. Again, I'm not saying that all of these colonial movements were entirely peaceful, but overwhelmingly so; we can say that those were peaceful expansions of culture and civilization to places that were less civilized and less cultured before.

Now, to the topic. I will return to the West as the ultimately superior civilization and I want to begin first with pre-state conflicts, that is, conflicts as they existed during the feudal age, essentially before 1500. In order to set the stage, remember that Europe—and that was one of the reasons for the uniqueness and for the development of Europe—was a highly decentralized place at this time, with tens of thousands of smaller or larger lords, princes, and kings. There existed at this time tens of thousands of people who owned a castle or a fortress and could say no to whomever wanted to plunder them or oppress them or tax them or whatever it was, because for a long time castles were indeed a very effective means of protecting yourself against any kind of enemy. And this protection that fortresses and castles constituted only gradually disappeared with the development of artillery, which appears for the very first time in 1325, but does not become a really relevant factor of warfare until about two hundred years later, that is in the 1500s. The fighting forces during this feudal age consisted, by and large, of mounted knights, which were quite expensive at this time. Horses, after all, compete with men for food and it was an expensive thing to own a horse and armor and weapons, and what all, to equip a fighting knight. And in addition, there were archers used in warfare. And from 1300 on, until about 1500, an important role was also played by pikemen. That was a strategy—developed in particular by the Swiss—of assembling large groups of people (in German they were called *Spießer Gewalthaufen*, "piker violence clusters" would be the translation), and these groups of pikemen were the first development that could stand up to mounted knights. Before this, mounted knights were the *non plus ultra* in terms of weaponry, until these massive groups of pikemen came into existence and they could take care of the mounted knights. These groups sometimes were three, four, or five thousand people in size, and they simply eliminated the horses. The fighters themselves were either the vassals of the lords, or the tenants of the lords. You recall during the feudal time there existed some sort of contractual relationship between the lords who owned the fortresses and offered protection, and the various tenants that they had for mutual assistance in cases of conflict.

Somewhat later, mercenary groups appeared, that is, groups that could be hired by whomever needed them for defensive or aggressive purposes. Fights were quite frequent at that time, but they were, as you can imagine, on a comparatively small scale and typically they were some sort of inheritance disputes. Who owns this place? Who owns this piece of land? And so forth. No army at that time exceeded 20,000 people, and most armies were significantly smaller than this. But what is important is that there existed certain rules about how to fight. Despite the fact that these fights were bloody, there existed something like knightly honor, and the knightly honor prescribed certain ways of proceeding and outlawed other ways. I want to read you a quote to this effect, by Stanislav Andreski, who I mentioned a few times before. He writes here that

> [a]t the height of the medieval civilization the wars were almost sporting matches: bloody, to be sure, but just as restricted by conventions. Let us look at one of the many examples of such a spirit. At the beginning of the fifteenth century Jagiello, the king of Poland and Lithuania, was fighting the Order of the Teutonic Knights. On one occasion, he found their army when it was crossing a river, and, although many of his warriors were eager to pounce upon the enemy, he restrained them because he thought that it was unworthy of a knight to attack the enemy who was not ready. When both armies finally met upon a fair ground they first engaged in parlays, during which the envoys of the Teutonic knights gave

> Jagiello two swords, thus mocking the inferior armament of his troops. Having slept overnight, each side celebrated a mass in its camp. When both sides were ready they signalled to each other by trumpeting, and then rushed into battle. As a rule, the medieval knights considered it unworthy of their honour to attack by surprise or pursue the defeated enemy. The knights who fell from their horses were usually spared and released for ransom.[1]

When mercenaries became used as soldiers, wars likewise were mostly bloodless battles. The mercenaries were a bunch of adventurers, international men. They were not united by any kind of ideology and their general attitude was that my enemy today might be my employer tomorrow, so I had better watch out to protect myself from being killed. Wait until those people who are my enemies maybe go bankrupt and have to give up, but in any case, avoid massive amounts of casualties. Again, to this effect, a quote from J.F.C. Fuller, a military historian who writes on mercenary warfare in fourteenth-century Italy. He writes,

> In Florence and in Milan and other ducal principalities, in their factional contests, their tyrants relied on highly trained professional mercenaries hired out by their *condottieri*, or contractor captains. These soldiers fought solely for profit; one year they might sell their services to one prince, and to his rival the next. For them war was a business as well as an art, in which the ransom of prisoners was more profitable than killing their employer's enemies. Because war was their trade, to prolong a war rather than to end it was clearly to their advantage.[2]

Hence, the historian Guicciardini writes:

---

[1]Stanislaw Andreski, *The Uses of Comparative Sociology* (Berkeley and Los Angeles: University of California Press, 1964), p. 111.

[2]J.F.C. Fuller, *The Conduct of War 1789–1961: A Study of the Impact of the French, Industrial, and Russian Revolutions on War and Its Conduct* (1961; London: Eyre and Spottiswoode, 2015), p. 1.

> They would spend the whole summer on the siege of a fortified place, so that wars were interminable, and campaigns ended with little or no loss of life, and by the end of the fifteenth century, such noted soldiers as the condottieri Paolo Vitelli and Prospero Colonna declared that "wars are won rather by industry and cunning than by the actual clash of arms."[3]

And of these soldiers Sir Charles Oman writes,

> The consequence of leaving the conduct of war in the hands of the great mercenary captains was that it came often to be waged as a mere tactical exercise or a game of chess, the aim being to manoeuvre the enemy into an impossible situation and then capture him, rather than to exhaust him by a series of costly battles. It was even suspected that condottieri, like dishonest pugilists, sometimes settled beforehand that they would draw the game. Battles when they did occur, were often bloodless affairs....Machiavelli cites cases of general actions in which there were only two or three men-at-arms slain, though the prisoners were to be numbered by the hundreds.[4]

From the sixteenth through the seventeenth century, essentially until the end of the Thirty Years' War in 1648, we see a change in warfare. We might call this period the period during which we do not have states fighting each other, but instead wars are conducted in order to create states. Remember, when I talked about the origin of the state, I explained how kings frequently tried to create the Hobbesian situation of war of all against all, in order to come out of this war as a state rather than as a feudal king who had to rely on voluntary contributions from his various vassals. These wars from the sixteenth to the seventeenth centuries were quite brutal. And just to document the thesis that these

---

[3]Cited in ibid., p. 2.

[4]Cited in ibid., pp. 2–3.

wars were wars that were used as instruments to the formation of states, here is a quote from a German historian, who writes,

> The years between 1500 and 1700 according to a recent study of the incidence of war in Europe, were "the most warlike in terms of the proportion of years of war under way (95 per cent), the frequency of war (nearly one every three years), and the average yearly duration, extent, and magnitude of war."[5]

This was the most warlike Europe had been up to this point; in 95 percent of the years, there was some war; on the average, every three years a new war was started, whereby the duration and the extent increased over time. In this case, up to the Thirty Years' War, these wars were not interstate wars, but they were state formation wars.

And these state formation wars fall right in the period of the Protestant Revolution. As I explained, the Protestant Revolution was precisely the event used by various princes to combine earthly and religious power and to establish themselves as state rulers rather than feudal kings. During this period, from 1500 to 1648, for the first time the wars take on an ideological connotation. What I mentioned before was that mercenaries had no ideology to fight for. The various feudal nobles fighting each other typically also had no ideological purposes in mind behind their fighting, but their reasons for fighting were more or less inheritance disputes, which tend to be settled by occupation; once you have occupied a certain territory, then the war's basically over. But these religious wars were ideologically motivated wars, and ideologically motivated wars (I'll come back to that later on when I talk about democratic wars) tend to be far more brutal than professional wars because they involve the participation of the masses.

Also, for the first time during this period, muskets were used. These had a range of about 200 meters, slightly more than 200 yards, but they were only able to shoot about once per minute. And artillery was used now, to a larger extent. In addition, from the seventeenth century

---

[5]Geoffrey Parker, *The Military Revolution: Military Innovation and the Rise of the West, 1500–1800*, 2d. ed. (Cambridge: Cambridge University Press, 1996), p. 1.

on, a combination of the piking strategy with the shooting musket was introduced by using bayonets. The ability to use artillery and muskets made it possible for the first time to defeat clusters of pikemen. Before then it was basically impossible to break them up. Now, through artillery fire and through the use of muskets, you could break up and spread out these clusters of pikemen and then be able to attack them. And also, the fortifications which, for a long time, had offered solid protection, became less and less protective because of the development of artillery. In response to the development of artillery, new types of fortifications were developed either in the form of triangles or in the form of stars and with some sort of water moats in front of them, in order to force the artillery to be placed at greater distances and to make the artillery less effective in crushing the walls of the fortifications.

The religious uprisings, which were initially stimulated by people like Luther and the various Protestant reforms, and the social chaos that resulted from them, as I said, was used by the various princes as a springboard for state formation and for forcing the smaller nobility into submission and accepting the rule and the taxing power of the larger lords. In addition, these religious wars were used by the princes to grab the substantial amounts of property that the Catholic Church owned; in some countries up to 30 percent of cultivated land was owned by the churches. Kings formed new alliances with national religions, and the old-style separation between church and state increasingly broke down and became more direct alliances between these two forces. At the end of the Thirty Years' War in 1648, the German territories, for instance, which had about 20 million people at the outset, had lost 8 million people as a result of this period of permanent state-formation wars. The modern state came into existence in Europe at the end of the Thirty Years' War.

Typically now, standing armies came into existence. Standing armies were, of course, far more expensive than hiring mercenaries here and there and then dismissing them again. So, the formation of standing armies requires, already, a certain amount of centralization of power and requires that taxing power exists on the part of the lords or kings. During the Thirty Years' War, for instance, there still existed some 1,500 independent *condottieri*, army leaders. All of these were now consolidated into standing armies. Either the independent mercenary companies were dissolved, or they were simply taken over as a state army and then had to be paid, of course, both during peacetime and wartime, which made them quite expensive. Nonetheless, even at this time, Europe remained highly decentralized. To give you an indication of this, even after the Thirty Years' War, Germany consisted of 234 countries, 51 free cities, and about 1,000 independent large manors owned by significant noble people.

After 1648, the next period of warfare begins, which we might call the period of monarchical warfare. And before I come to characterize this period of monarchical warfare, let me present some theoretical arguments that help us understand the development that results now, after the Thirty Years' War. First, we should recognize that institutions such as states show a natural aggressiveness. The explanation is very simple. If you have to fund your own aggressive ventures yourself, out of your own pocket, that will somewhat curtail your natural inclination to fight other people, because you have to pay for it yourself. On the other hand, if you imagine that if I want to fight some of you guys and I can tax him or him or him and ask them to support me in my fighting endeavors, then whatever my initial aggressive impulses might be, are certainly stimulated because I can externalize the cost of war onto other people. I don't have to bear the cost myself. Other people have to bear the cost. This explains why institutions that have the power to tax, and also institutions that have the power to print money, in later ages, have financial abilities that make it more likely that they go to war than you would go to war if the power to tax was lacking or the power to print money was lacking on your part.

We can also see that states, because they compete with each other for population, do not like to see people moving from one state to another state. After all, every individual that moves from one place to another means there is one taxpayer less here, and your opponent gets one taxpayer more. The high degree of decentralization that existed in Europe went hand in hand with a high degree of regional mobility, people moving from territories that were more oppressive to territories that were less oppressive, and this then causes automatic rivalries between the different states and leads frequently to war. And we can say that this competition between states, in contrast to the competition of General Motors against Ford or Toyota against Honda or whatever, that the competition between states is an eliminative competition. It is possible that Ford and Toyota and Honda and GM can live side-by-side, coexist side by side until the end of history. However, there can, in any given territory, be only one institution that is entitled to tax and pass laws. There cannot be free competition in a territory in terms of taxing power and legislative power. If everybody could tax everybody, there would be nothing left to be taxed, and if everybody could make laws, chaos would break out.

The competition between states is eliminative in the sense that in any given territory, there can only exist one taxing authority and one monopolist of legislation and we should expect that wars will by and large lead to a tendency to concentration. That is, more and more of these small states are eliminated and the territories of states become gradually larger and larger.

And we can also quickly address and resolve the question as to who is about to win and who is about to lose in these types of battles. If you assume that states were initially of roughly equal size with roughly equal populations, then we recognize some sort of paradox, that is, that those states that treat their populations nicer, more liberal states, so to speak, are the states that have a more prosperous civil society than those states that mistreat their populations, because if you are liberal to your population, less oppressive to your population, they tend to be more productive. And after all, in a war, in order to conduct a war, especially a war that lasts for a while, that requires that you have a productive population. People have to continue working, have to continue making weaponry and feeding the soldiers, etc., and those territories, those state territories that oppress their population, tend to be also poor places that have fewer resources on which to draw in the conduct of war. We would expect that as a tendency, more liberal states will, at least in the long run, defeat less liberal states, wiping them out and enlarging their territory at the expense of these less liberal states.

You can see, however, that there is a limitation to this tendency. That is, the larger the territories become, the more difficult it becomes for people to move from one territory to another. At the conceivable end point of the process of concentration we have a one world state, the possibility for people to vote with their feet entirely disappears. Wherever you go, the same tax and regulation structure applies. The implication of that is with larger and larger territories, the initial reason for state rulers to be comparatively moderate in their taxing and regulation policy to their own population, in order to be successful in wars, this initial motive disappears more and more, the larger the territories become, and the more difficult voting with your feet becomes. So, we can recognize some sort of dialectic process. Initially, you want to be relatively liberal in order to expand your territory. The more successful you become in expanding your territory, the less important becomes the motive to be liberal to our own population, because voting with your feet becomes ever more difficult.

Jumping ahead for a moment, this sort of paradox, that is, that liberal states tend to be more aggressive in their foreign policy, is nicely illustrated, in a way, by comparing the United States and the former Soviet Union. There's no doubt that the former Soviet Union was an extremely oppressive state internally, with the result being that they had a basket case economy, and the United States, on the other hand, being a comparatively nice country, was a very prosperous economy. And if we now look at the foreign policy of these two countries, we find what some people consider to be a curious result, but which I think can be easily explained. We find that the Soviet Union engaged in comparatively few imperialist ventures. And those imperialist ventures that they engaged in were usually in second-, third-, and fourth-rate places because they knew precisely that their economy was so weak that they could not take on a highly developed country, due to lack of resources needed in the conduct of war. Keep in mind that the main territorial gains that the Soviet Union achieved were territorial gains that were granted to it by the United States as a result of various agreements during World War II. All of Eastern Europe was given to the Soviet Union by the Americans; it would not have been possible for the Soviet Union to take over all of these places if they had to fight the United States to the hilt. The leadership of the United States actually ordered some of the generals, like General Patton, to withdraw, and prevented him from marching further to the east, from taking over places like Prague and so forth, to prevent communism from spreading to the West. So, the main territorial gains of the Soviet Union can hardly be described as the result of their internal imperialist desires.

But if you compare this with the foreign policy of the United States, you find that the United States has, in fact, in every single year, been engaged in various sorts of imperialist ventures. And the explanation for this is precisely that the United States did that because they knew as a result of their internal resources, because of their internal wealth, they would likely become winners, whereas the Soviet Union full well knew that they would not be capable of waging a successful war against highly industrialized countries. That was not the result of the goodness of the hearts of Gorbachev and Brezhnev and their other leaders. Quite to the contrary, I admit that these were evil people and that the Soviet Union was, so to speak, the Evil Empire, all of this is perfectly correct. Nonetheless, there is a rational explanation for why they were reluctant in their imperialist desires and why the United States, precisely because it is more liberal internally, was more aggressive as far as its external policy is concerned.

Now, back to monarchical wars, before the backdrop of these theoretical considerations. Recall that kings, princely rulers, regard their country as their own property. Even in wars which are typically motivated by inheritance disputes, that is, which are non-ideologically motivated wars, even during these wars, kings and princes have incentive to preserve the territories that they try to take over—because after all, they regard themselves as the owner of the capital stock represented by these provinces and this then leads to a relatively civilized form of warfare during the monarchical age. And again, some quotes, to this effect, referring to monarchical state wars and showing the moderation of these types of non-ideological, territorially motivated wars. First, a quote from a military historian, Arne Røksund. He says,

> On the continent, commerce, travel, cultural and learned intercourse went on in wartime almost unhindered. The wars were the King's wars; the role of the good citizen was to pay his taxes, and sound political economy dictated that he should be left alone to make the money out of which to pay those taxes. He was required to participate neither in the decisions out of which wars arose, nor to take part in them once they broke out, unless prompted by a spirit of useful adventures. These matters

> were purely royal matters and the concern of the sovereign alone.[6]

And a Swiss-Italian historian, Guglielmo Ferrero, writes of the wars during the eighteenth century:

> War became limited and circumscribed by a system of precise rules. It was definitely regarded as a kind of single combat between the two armies, the civil population being merely spectators. Pillage, requisitions and acts of violence against the population were forbidden in the home country as well as in the enemy country. Each army established depots in its rear in carefully chosen towns, shifting them as it moved about.... Conscription existed only in rudimentary and sporadic form....Soldiers being scarce and hard to find, everything was done to ensure their quality by long, patient and meticulous training, but as this was costly, it rendered them very valuable, and it was necessary to let as few be killed as possible. Having to economize their men, generals tried to avoid fighting battles. The object of warfare was the execution of skillful maneuvers and not the annihilation of the adversary; a campaign without battles and without loss of life, a victory obtained by a clever combination of movements, was considered the crowning achievement of this art, the ideal pattern of perfection....It was avarice and calculation that made war more humane....War became a kind of game between sovereigns. A war was a game with its rules and its stakes—a territory, an inheritance, a throne, a treaty. The loser paid, but a just proportion was always kept between the value of the stake and the risks to be taken, and the parties were always on guard against the kind of obstinacy which makes a player lose his head.

[6]Arne Røksund, "The Jeune École," in Rolf Hobson and Tom Kristiansen, eds., *Navies in Northern Waters* (London: Routledge, 2004), p. 139.

> They tried to keep the game in hand and to know when to stop.[7]

We come back, on a slightly larger scale, to the form of warfare that existed during the age of knights. The difference being here essentially that the armies are, of course, of far larger size than they were at this earlier age.

Now comes the next transformation in the conduct of war, and that is the transformation from monarchical wars to democratic wars, to national wars. I spoke about this transition from monarchy to democracy previously. This transition begins with the French Revolution, is then interrupted, to a certain extent, after the defeat of Napoleon in 1815, until 1914 with the outbreak of World War I, and it resumes in World War I and after up to the present. But, the first new experience is indeed the French Revolution.

The French Revolution represents, in a way, a return to these religious types of wars that I mentioned earlier. It is an ideologically motivated event. The king is killed and instead, some high-floating ideals become prominent: liberty, fraternity, and the glory of the nation and things of this nature. The right to vote is introduced, and as people could not vote before and always said, "If the king goes to war, we have nothing to do with the state, this is the king's state, we don't get involved in the king's wars," now the argument was turned around, saying, "Now all of a sudden we give you a stake in the state, you participate in the state, you elect, you have the right to elect representatives, etc., and as a consequence you also have to serve in the state's wars." Revolutionary France now introduces for the first time what had existed in rudimentary form in the past, but in very rudimentary form—kings had tried to introduce a draft, but were typically unsuccessful. For the first time was seen now, during the French Revolution, and in particular after Napoleon comes to power, the draft, a mass draft. All the people of the French population are somehow made participants in the war. There exists no clear-cut distinction anymore

---

[7]Guglielmo Ferrero, *Peace and War* (Freeport, NJ: Books for Libraries Press, 1969), pp. 5–7.

between combatants and noncombatants; the resources of the entire nation are put at the disposal of the warring armies.

Since it is no longer inheritance disputes that motivate wars, but ideological differences (i.e., the hatred against monarchs, the desire to spread liberty, whatever that means), it becomes extremely difficult to stop wars. If you have nonideologically motivated wars with territorial objectives, then once you have reached your territorial objective, the reason for the war is over. Once you have ideological motives, you want to make the world safe for liberty or nowadays for democracy, you are never quite sure if you actually reached your goal. Maybe these people just pretend that they have become democrats or Catholics or Protestants, and the only way that you are really sure that you succeeded in your conversion is, of course, to kill as many as possible. Then you know for sure that they don't adhere to their old wrong beliefs anymore.

And, of course, there are no borders. How far should you extend your war? If you liberate Germany and turn to make that a free country, what about Poland? They have not been freed yet and if you win Poland, then what about Russia? Russia needs to be freed as well. Then you turn to the South, Egypt needs to be freed and Spain needs to be freed. The world is a wide place and all of them are yearning for freedom, of course, so it becomes impossible to ever end a war. So, war becomes total war. And then there is the size of the armies: the biggest armies before Napoleon were about 400,000 under Louis XIV, which was considered a huge army. The armies under Napoleon were well above a million. Now I quote, from Fuller and from Howard, to illustrate this change in warfare that began with the French Revolution. First, Howard. He says,

> Once the state ceased to be regarded as the "property" of dynastic princes…and became instead the instrument of powerful forces dedicated to such abstract concepts as Liberty, or Nationality, or Revolution, which enabled large numbers of the population to see in that state the embodiment of some absolute Good, for which no price was too high, no sacrifice too great

> to pay; then the temperate and indecisive contests of the rococo age appeared as absurd anachronisms.[8]

And another quote,

> Truly enough, a new era had begun, the era of national wars, of wars which were to assume a maddening pace; for those wars were destined to throw into the fight all the resources of the nation; they were to set themselves the goal, not a dynastic interest, not of the conquest or possession of a province, but the defense or the propagation of philosophical ideas in the first place, next of the principles of independence, of unity, of immaterial advantages of various kinds. Lastly they staked upon the issue the interests and fortune of every individual private. Hence, the rising of passions, that is the elements of force, hitherto in the main unused.[9]

And another set of quotes, very revealing, from J.F.C. Fuller.

> The influence of the spirit of nationality, that is, of democracy, on war, was profound....[It] emotionalized war and, consequently, brutalized it....In the eighteenth century, wars were largely the occupation of kings, courtiers and gentlemen. Armies lived on their depots, they interfered as little as possible with the people, and as soldiers were paid out of the king's privy purse they were too costly to be thrown away lightly on mass attacks. The change came about with the French Revolution, *sanscoulottism* replaced courtiership, and as armies became more and more the instruments of the people, not only did they grow in size but in ferocity. National armies fight nations, royal armies fight their like, the first obey a mob—always demented, the sec-

[8]Michael Howard, *War in European History* (1976; Cambridge: Cambridge University Press, 2009), chap. 5.

[9]Ferdinand Foch, *The Principles of War* (1903), cited in J.F.C. Fuller, *The Conduct of War, 1789–1961*, p. 34.

> ond a king—generally sane....All this developed out of the French Revolution, which also gave to the world conscription—herd warfare, and the herd coupling with finance and commerce has begotten new realms of war. For when once the whole nation fights, then is the whole national credit become available for the purposes of war.[10]

And further on the same topic:

> Conscription changed the basis of warfare. Hitherto, soldiers had been costly, now they were cheap; battles had been avoided, now they were sought, and however heavy were the losses, they could rapidly be made good by the muster-roll....From August (of 1793, when the Parliament of the French Republic decreed universal compulsory military service) onward, not only was war to become more and more unlimited, but finally, total. In the fourth decade of the twentieth century, life was held so cheaply that the massacre of civilian populations on wholesale lines became as accepted a strategic aim as battles were in previous wars. In 150 years conscription had led the world back to tribal barbarism.[11]

Now, there was, as I said, a small pause after the defeat of Napoleon. The wars that were fought in Europe during the nineteenth century after Napoleon's defeat, such as the war, for instance, of Germany against France in 1870–71, was again, a traditional monarchical war, almost harmless. The German officers resided in French hotels and paid their bills whereas the French military asked the hotel to wait for payment until later dates. There was practically no involvement of the civilian population whatsoever. The only major exception in the nineteenth century from this return to civilized warfare, if we can call warfare civilized at all, was the American War of Southern Independence. And this, again, was a typical democratic war; so much for the

[10]J.F.C. Fuller, *War and Western Civilization, 1832–1932* (London: Duckworth, 1932), p. 26.

[11]J.F.C. Fuller, *The Conduct of War, 1789–1961*, pp. 33, 35.

thesis that democracies do not fight each other and democracies are somehow better suited to creating peace. The only democratic war in the nineteenth century was, again, the only ideologically motivated war and the American Civil War was, up until this point, unsurpassed in terms of brutality. It was at least as brutal as the religious wars had been many centuries before and as you all know, more Americans were killed in that war than all the Americans who died in World War I and in World War II as well.

This war, for the first time, brings to bear all modern weaponry: machine guns and telegraphs and railroads and steamships and rifles of great accuracy over some 1,000 meters. And then, this type of warfare, of which the American war was a typical example, and the French one, the Napoleonic wars before, this type of warfare then continues with World War I, particularly after the entry of the United States, which was much earlier than the official entry.

The United States was, from the very beginning, due to British propaganda, on the side of the Western forces. The entry of the United States into the war was much facilitated by two of our most beloved institutions, one of which was the introduction of the income tax in 1913 and the other one is the founding of the Federal Reserve System in the same year, both of which, of course, facilitated greatly the possibility of a country like the United States carrying on a war far away from its own shores. Just to give you some ballpark idea, for instance, the reserve requirements for the central bank during the war were lowered from 20 percent before the war to 10 percent during the war, which basically implies a doubling of the money supply, which, of course, enables greatly the financing of adventures such as this. And again, with the entry of the United States early on, what began as some sort of traditional European monarchical war and could have ended easily by 1916—there were various peace initiatives underway, one by the pope and another by the Austrian emperor Karl—this war then became an ideological war, as you know, the war to "make the world safe for democracy." As my friend Kuehnelt-Leddihn noted, it would be more appropriate to say, "We should not make the world safe for democracy. We should make the world safe from democracy."

And as a result of this ideologically motivated war, the war ended, of course, not with a mutually face-saving compromise peace, but ended with a completely ridiculous demand for total and complete and unconditional surrender, and forcing the Germans and the Austrians to accept sole exclusive guilt for the war, despite the fact that even nowadays, there are very few historians who would maintain that the war was exclusively caused by Austria or Germany. If anything, the most guilty parties, in my judgment, were the Russians, by encouraging the Serbs not to give in to the relatively moderate demands of the Austrians—and the Russians would not have done that, if they had not had some sort of alliance with the British encouraging the Russians to behave the way they did. So, not being an historian, just being an amateur historian, I would blame Russia and England more so than Austria and Germany for the war. But in any case, this war ended with a disastrous peace treaty, which then implied already the seeds for World War II. In many ways, World War II can be considered to be just the continuation of the first one, with a brief interlude. As a matter of fact, one of the better-known German historians, Hans Nolte, has written a book with the title that this was another Thirty Years' War, that is, describing history as if World War I almost automatically led up to World War II.

And of World War II, we know that the exact same thing happened. It was an ideologically motivated war, with America siding with Stalin. Stalin, who was a bigger killer than Hitler by far, and not only no longer respected in any way the distinction between combatants and noncombatants, wiping out huge masses of the civilian population at points when the outcome of the war was long decided, just for the mere purpose of instilling terror in the population, and then handing over all of middle and Eastern Europe to Communist rule.

I want to end with a long quote from Mises, which does not deal directly with the question whether societies' natural orders can defend themselves against enemy states, but it can be read as an indirect statement on this question. Can free societies defend themselves against hordes of barbarians trying to occupy them? And the upshot of this longer quotation is, yes, it is precisely the internal coherence, the integration economically and monetarily of highly civilized societies that can withstand the onslaught of even the most barbarian invasions. Mises says here this:

We must reject *a priori* any assumption that historical evolution is provided with a goal by any "intention" or "hidden plan" of Nature, such as Kant imagined and Hegel and Marx had in mind; but we cannot avoid the inquiry whether a principle might not be found to demonstrate that continuous social growth is inevitable. The first principle that offers itself to our attention is the principle of natural selection. More highly developed societies attain greater material wealth than the less highly developed; therefore, they have more prospect of preserving their members from misery and poverty. They are also better equipped to defend themselves from the enemy. One must not be misled by the observation that richer and more civilized nations were often crushed in war by nations less wealthy and civilized. Nations in an advanced stage of social evolution have always been able at least to resist a superior force of less developed nations. It is only decaying nations, civilizations inwardly disintegrated, which have fallen prey to nations on the upgrade. Where a more highly organized society has succumbed to the attack of a less developed people the victors have in the end become culturally submerged, accepting the economic and social order and even the language and faith of the conquered race.

The superiority of the more highly developed societies lies not only in their material welfare, but also quantitatively in the number of their members and qualitatively in the greater solidity of their internal structure. For this, precisely, is the key to higher social development: the widening of the social range, the inclusion in the division of labor of more human beings and its stronger grip on each individual. The more highly developed society differs from the less developed in the closer union of its members; this precludes the violent solution of internal conflict and forms externally a close defensive front against any enemy. In less developed societies, where the social bond is still weak, and between the separate parts of which there exists a confederation for the purposes of war rather than true solidarity based on joint work and economic cooperation—disagreement breaks out more easily and more quickly than in highly developed societies. For the military confederation has no firm and lasting hold upon its members. By its very nature it is merely a temporary bond which is upheld by the prospect of momentary advantage, but dissolves as soon as the enemy has been defeated and the scramble for the booty sets in. In fighting against the less developed societies the more developed ones have always found that their greatest advantage lay in the lack of unity in the enemy's ranks. Only temporarily do the nations in a lower state of organization manage to cooperate for great military enterprises. Internal disunity has always dispersed their armies quickly. Take for example the Mongol raids on the Central European civilization of the thirteenth century or the efforts of the Turks to penetrate into the West. The superiority of the industrial over the military type of society, to use Herbert Spencer's expression, consists largely in the fact that associations which are merely military always fall to pieces through internal disunity.[12]

[12]Ludwig von Mises, *Socialism: An Economic and Sociological Analysis* (Auburn, AL: Ludwig von Mises Institute, 2009), pp. 306–07.

LECTURE 10

Strategy, Secession, Privatization, and the Prospects of Liberty

THE UPSHOT OF ALL MY lectures is that the institution of the state represents somehow an error and a deviation from the normal and natural cause of civilization. And all errors are costly and have to be paid for. This is most obvious with errors concerning the laws of nature. If a person errs regarding the laws of nature, this person will not be able to reach his own goals. However, because a failure to do so must be borne by each individual, there prevails in the area of the natural sciences a universal desire to learn and to eliminate and correct one's errors. On the other hand, moral errors are costly also, but unlike in the case of the natural sciences, the cost of moral errors may not be paid for by each and every person that commits this error.

For instance, take the error that we have talked about here in detail, take the error of believing that one agency, and only one agency, the state, has the right to tax and to ultimate decision-making. That is, that there must be different and unequal laws applying to masters and serfs, to the taxers and the taxed, to the legislators and the legislated. A society that believes in this error can, of course, exist and last, as we all know, but this error must be paid for too. But, the interesting thing is that not everyone holding this error must pay for it equally. Rather, some people will have to pay for the error, while others, maybe the agents of the state, actually benefit from the same error. Because of this, in this case, it would be mistaken to assume that there exists a universal desire to learn and to correct one's error. Quite to the contrary, in this case, it will have to be assumed that some people instead of learning and promoting the truth, actually have a constant motive to lie, that is, to maintain and promote falsehoods, even if they themselves recognize them as such.

Let me explain this in a little bit more detail and repeat some of the basic insights that I tried to convey during these lectures. Once you accept the principle of government, namely that there must be a judicial monopoly and the power to tax, once you accept this principle incorrectly as a just principle, then any idea or any notion of restraining or limiting government power and safeguarding individual liberty and property becomes illusory. Rather, under monopolistic auspices, the price of justice and protection will continually rise, and the quality of justice and protection will continually fall. A tax-funded protection agency is a contradiction in terms. That is, it is an expropriating property protector. And such an institution will inevitably lead to more taxes and ever less protection, even if, as some classical liberals demand, a government were to limit its activities exclusively to the protection of preexisting private property rights. Then immediately the further question would arise, "How much security to produce and how many resources to spend on this particular good of protection?" And motivated, like everyone else, by self-interest, but equipped with the unique power to tax, a government agent's answer will invariably be the same. That is, to maximize expenditures on protection (and, as you can imagine, almost the entire wealth of a nation can, in principle, be expended on protection. We just have to equip everyone with a personal bodyguard and tank with a flamethrower on top), and at the same time to minimize what they are supposed to do, that is, the production of protection. The more money you can spend and the less you must work for this money, the better off you are.

Now, in addition, a judicial monopoly will inevitably lead to a steady deterioration in the quality of justice and protection. If no one can appeal to justice except to the government, justice will invariably be perverted in favor of government, constitutions, and supreme courts notwithstanding. After all, constitutions and supreme courts are state constitutions and state agencies, and whatever limitations to state activities these institutions might find or contain, is invariably decided by agents of the very institution that is under consideration. It is easily predictable that the definition of property and the definition of protection will continually be altered and the range of jurisdiction expanded to the government's advantage, until ultimately the notion of universal and immutable human rights, and in particular property rights, will disappear and will be replaced by that of law as government-made legislation and rights as government-given grants to people.

Now, the results are all before our own eyes and everyone can see them. The tax load that is imposed on property owners and producers has continually increased, making even the economic burden of slaves and serfs seem moderate in comparison. Government debt, and hence future tax obligations, has risen to breathtaking heights. Every detail of private life, of property, of trade, and of contract is regulated by ever higher mountains of paper laws. Yet, the only task that the government was ever supposed to assume, that of protecting life and property, it does not perform too well. To the contrary, the higher the expenditures on social welfare and national security have risen, the more our private property rights have been eroded, the more our property has been expropriated, confiscated, destroyed, and depreciated. The more paper laws have been produced, the more legal uncertainty and moral hazard has been created, and the more lawlessness has displaced law and order. Instead of protecting us from domestic crime and from foreign aggression, our government, which is equipped with enormous stockpiles of weapons of mass destruction, aggresses against ever new Hitlers and suspected Hitlerite sympathizers, anywhere and everywhere outside of its own territory. In short, while we have become ever more helpless, impoverished, threatened, and insecure, our state rulers have become increasingly more corrupt, arrogant, and dangerously armed.

Now, what can we do about all this? Let me begin by first pointing out something that I have mentioned already before, that is, we have to recognize that states, as powerful and as invincible as they might seem, ultimately owe their existence to ideas, and since ideas can in principle change instantaneously, states can be brought down and crumble practically overnight too. The representatives of the state are always and everywhere only just a small minority of the population over which they rule. The reason for this, as I explained, is as simple as it is fundamental. One hundred parasites can live comfortable lives if they suck out the lifeblood of thousands of productive hosts, but thousands of parasites cannot live comfortably off a host population of just a few hundred. Yet, if government agents are merely a small minority of the population, how can they enforce their will on this population and get away with it? The answer given by Rothbard, de La Boétie, Hume, and Mises is only by virtue of the voluntary cooperation of the majority of the subject population with the state.

Yet, how can the state secure such cooperation? And the answer is, only because and insofar as the majority of the population believes in the legitimacy of state rule, in the necessity of the institution of the state. This is not to say that the majority of the population must agree with every single state measure. In fact, it may well believe that many state policies are mistakes or even despicable. However, the majority of the population must believe in the justice of the institution of the state as such, and hence that even if a particular government goes wrong or makes particular mistakes, that these mistakes are merely accidents, which must be accepted and tolerated in view of some greater good provided by the institution of government. That is, people believe in the accident theory of government error instead of seeing that there is a systematic reason behind all of this. Yet, how can the majority of the population be brought to believe this accident theory? And the answer is, with the help of the intellectuals. In the old days, that meant trying to mold an alliance between the state and the church. In modern times, far more effectively, this means through the nationalization or the socialization of education, through state-run and state-subsidized schools and universities. The market demand for intellectual services, in particular in the area of the humanities and the social sciences, is not exactly high and also not exactly stable and secure. Intellectuals would be at the mercy of the values and choices of the masses and the masses are generally uninterested in intellectual and philosophical concerns. The state, on the other hand, as Rothbard has noted, accommodates their typically overinflated egos and is willing to offer the intellectuals a warm, secure, and permanent berth in its apparatus, a secure income and the panoply of prestige. And indeed, the modern democratic state in particular has created a massive oversupply of intellectuals.

Now, this accommodation does not guarantee correct statist thinking of course. Also, as generally overpaid as intellectuals are, they will continue to complain how little their "oh so important" work is appreciated by the powers that be. But it certainly helps in reaching the correct statist conclusions if one realizes that without the state, that is, without the institutions of taxation and legislation, one might be out of work entirely, and might have to try his hand at the mechanics of gas pump operation instead of concerning himself with such pressing problems as alienation and equity and exploitation and the deconstruction of gender and sex roles or the culture of the Eskimos, the Hopis and the Zulus. And even if one feels underappreciated by this or that incumbent government, intellectuals still realize that help can only come from another government, and certainly not from an intellectual assault on the legitimacy of the very institution of government as such. Thus, it is hardly surprising that, as a matter of empirical fact, the overwhelming majority of contemporary intellectuals are far-out lefties, and that even most conservative or free market intellectuals, such as, for instance, Milton Friedman or Friedrich von Hayek, are fundamentally and philosophically also statists.

Now, from this insight to the importance of ideas and the role of intellectuals as bodyguards of the state and of statism, it follows that the most decisive role in the process of liberation, that is, the restoration of justice and morality, must fall on the shoulders of what one might call anti-intellectual intellectuals. Yet, how can such anti-intellectual intellectuals possibly succeed in delegitimizing the state in public opinion, especially if the overwhelming majority of their colleagues are statists and will do everything in their power to isolate and discredit them as extremists and crackpots? The first thing is this. Because one must reckon with the vicious opposition from one's colleagues, and in order to withstand this criticism and to shrug it off, it is of utmost importance to ground one's own case, not just in economics and in utilitarian arguments, but in ethics and moral arguments, because only moral convictions provide one with the courage and the strength needed in ideological battle. Few people are inspired and willing to accept sacrifices if what they are opposed to is mere error and waste. More inspiration and more courage can be drawn from knowing that one is engaged in fighting evil and lies.

The second point I want to emphasize is this. It is equally important to recognize that one does not need to convert one's colleagues, that is, that one does not need to persuade mainstream intellectuals. As Thomas Kuhn has shown, in particular, converting one's colleagues is a rare enough event, even in the natural sciences. In the social sciences, conversions among established intellectuals from previously held views are almost unheard of. Now, instead, one should concentrate one's efforts on the not yet intellectually committed young, whose idealism makes them particularly receptive to moral arguments and to moral rigorism. And likewise one should circumvent, as far as this is possible, pure academic institutions and reach out to the general public, which has some generally healthy anti-intellectual prejudices into which one can easily tap.

The third point is—and this makes me return to the importance of a moral attack on the state—it is essential to recognize that there can be no compromise on the level of theory. To be sure, one should not refuse to cooperate with people whose views are ultimately mistaken and confused, provided that their objectives can be classified clearly and unambiguously as a step in the right direction of a destatization of society. For instance, one would not want to refuse cooperation with people who seek to introduce a flat income tax of 10 percent. However, we would not want to cooperate with those who want to combine this measure with an increased sales tax in order to achieve revenue neutrality, for instance. Under no circumstances should such cooperation lead to compromising one's principles. Either taxation is just or it isn't, and once it is admitted that it is just, how is one then to oppose any increase in it? And the answer is, of course, that then one has no argument left over. Put differently, compromise, on the level of theory, as we find it, for instance, among moderate free marketeers, such as Hayek or Friedman, or even among some so-called minarchists, is not only philosophically flawed, but it is also practically ineffective and even counterproductive. Their ideas can be, and in fact are, easily coopted and incorporated by the state rulers and by the statist ideology. In fact, how often do we hear nowadays from statists, in defense of a statist agenda, cries such as "even Hayek or Friedman says such and such" or "not even Hayek or Friedman would propose anything like this"?

Now, personally, Friedman and Hayek might not be happy about this, but there is no denying that their work lends itself to this very purpose, and hence, that they willy-nilly actually contributed to the continued and unabating power of the state. In other words, theoretical compromise and gradualism will only lead to the perpetuation of the falsehood, the evils, and the lies of statism, and only theoretical purism, radicalism, and intransigence can and will lead first to gradual practical reform and improvement and possibly also to final victory. Accordingly, as an anti-intellectual intellectual, in the Rothbardian sense, one can never be satisfied with criticizing various government follies. Although one might have to begin with criticizing such follies, one must always proceed from there onto a fundamental attack on the institution of the state as such, as a moral outrage, and on its representatives as moral as well as economic frauds, liars, and imposters, or as emperors without clothes. In particular, one must never hesitate to strike at the very heart of the legitimacy of the state and its alleged indispensable role as producer of private protection and security. I have already shown how ridiculous this claim is on theoretical grounds. How can an agency that may expropriate private property possibly claim to be a protector of private property?

But, hardly less important is it to attack the legitimacy of the state on empirical grounds, that is, to point out and hammer away on the subject that after all, states, which are supposed to protect us, are the very institution responsible for some estimated 170 million deaths in peacetime in the twentieth century alone; that is probably more than the victims of private crime in all of human history. And this number of victims of private crimes from which government did not protect us would have been even much lower if governments everywhere and at all times had not undertaken constant efforts to disarm its own citizens so that the governments, in turn, could become ever more effective killing machines. Instead of treating politicians with respect, then, one's criticism of them should be significantly stepped up. Almost to a man—there might be a few exceptions—almost to a man, politicians are not only thieves, but in fact, mass murderers or at least assistants of mass murderers. And how do they dare to demand our respect and loyalty?

But, will a sharp and distinct logical radicalization bring about the results that we want to achieve? In this, I have very little doubt. Indeed, only radical and in fact, radically simple ideas can possibly stir the emotions of the dour and indolent masses and delegitimize government in their eyes. Let me quote Hayek to this effect and from this, you realize that even a guy who is fundamentally muddled and mistaken can have very important insights, and that we can learn very much also from those people who do not agree totally with us.

> We must make the building of a free society once more an intellectual adventure, a deed of courage. What we lack is a liberal Utopia, a program which seems neither a mere defense of things as they are nor a diluted kind of socialism, but a truly liberal radicalism which does not spare the susceptibilities of the mighty (including the trade unions), which is not too severely practical and which does not confine itself to what appears today as politically possible. We need intellectual leaders who are prepared to resist the blandishments of power and influence and who are willing to work for an ideal, however small may be the prospects of its early realization. They must be men who are willing to stick to principles and to fight for their full realization, however remote. Free trade or the freedom of opportunity are ideas which still may arouse the imaginations of large numbers, but a mere "reasonable freedom of trade" or a mere "relaxation of controls" are neither intellectually respectable nor likely to inspire any enthusiasm.
>
> Unless we can make the philosophical foundations of a free society once more a living intellectual issue and its implementation a task which challenges the ingenuity and imagination of our liveliest minds, the prospects of freedom are indeed dark. But if we can

> regain that belief in the power of ideas which was a mark of liberalism at its greatest, the battle is not lost.[1]

Now, Hayek, of course, did not heed his own advice to provide us with a consistent and inspiring theory. His utopia as developed, for instance, in his *Constitution of Liberty*, is instead the uninspiring vision of the Swedish welfare state. But, it is Rothbard, above all, who has done what Hayek recognized as necessary for the renewal of classical liberalism, that is, he had given us an inspiring utopia, something that is based on morals and is capable of invigorating, especially the young and intellectually uncommitted.

Now, let me end by also trying to offer some sort of inspiring utopia for intermediate goals, goals before we reach a fully destatized society. You realize that if we follow the logic of the state to its ultimate conclusion, then what we must demand is a world state, because as long as there is no world state, then according to the statist ideology itself, there will be perpetual war among states because they are, *vis-à-vis* each other, in a state of anarchy. The only ultimate solution would be that of a world state. This is precisely the vision that our leaders try to propagate. Of course, a world state under control of the United States, to be more precise, but in any case, it requires a world state. Instead, the utopia, the intermediate utopia that I would suggest takes its cues from what we have learned from the Middle Ages and from the peculiar organization of Europe which was responsible for the unique success of the Western world, that is, the quasi-anarchistic structure, the highly decentralized structure of Europe. What we can propose as an intermediate goal, which I think is more inspiring than the world state, is the view of a world composed of tens of thousands of Monacos and Liechtensteins and Swiss Cantons and Singapores and Hong Kongs and San Marinos and whatever small entities nowadays still exist. Recall, if we have a large number of small political entities, each of these entities will have to be relatively moderate and nice to its population, otherwise, people will simply run away from it.

---

[1]Friedrich A. Hayek, *The Constitution of Liberty* (1978; Chicago: University of Chicago Press, 2005), p. 384.

Second, each one of these small units will have to engage almost necessarily in an open free trade policy. The United States, as a large country, can engage in protectionist measures because it has a large internal market. Even if it were to stop trading with the rest of the world, the United States population would experience a significant decline in standards of living, but people would not die. On the other hand, imagine Liechtenstein or Monaco or San Marino declaring no more trade, no more free trade with the outside world, or Hong Kong, places such as this. Then, of course, it would take a week or two and the entire population in these places would be wiped out. So, small units must, in order to avoid starving to death or losing, in particular, their most productive individuals in no time, must engage in classical liberal policies.

In addition, a large number of very small units would have to give up, of necessity, the institution of paper money because there cannot be tens of thousands of different paper monies issued by tens of thousands of different political units. We would basically be back to a system of barter if we were to do this. The smaller the units are, the greater is the pressure, in fact, that we will return also to a commodity money standard, which is entirely independent of government control.

What I would recommend, in particular, for the United States and so forth, is to realize that democracy will not abolish itself. The masses like to loot other people's property. They will not give up the right to continue doing this. However, there are still, in the United States and in many other places, small islands of reasonable people, and it is possible that on small local levels, some people, some natural authorities can gain enough influence in order to induce them to secede from their central state. And if they do so, and if that accelerates, if it happens at many places simultaneously, it will be almost impossible for the central state to crush a movement such as this. Because in order to crush a movement such as this, again, public opinion has to be in favor of this and it would be difficult to persuade the public to attack to kill, to destroy small places that have done nothing other than to declare that they wish to be independent of the United States.

Index

(Compiled by Sven Thommesen)

Mises Institute
518 West Magnolia Avenue
Auburn, Alabama 36832
mises.org

Made in the USA
Monee, IL
16 January 2022